W9-AZS-998

Chronic Illness

LIVING WITH A SPECIAL NEED

LIVING WITH A SPECIAL NEED

Chronic Illness

AUTUMN LIBAL

MASON CREST

Mason Crest
450 Parkway Drive, Suite D
Broomall, PA 19008
www.masoncrest.com

Printed in the United States of America.

Series ISBN: 978-1-4222-3027-5
ISBN: 978-1-4222-3032-9
ebook ISBN: 978-1-4222-8817-7

Library of Congress Cataloging-in-Publication Data

Libal, Autumn.
  Chronic illness / Autumn Libal.
     pages cm. — (Living with a special need)
  Includes index.
  Audience: 12
  Audience: 7 to 8
  ISBN 978-1-4222-3032-9 (hardback) — ISBN 978-1-4222-3027-5 (series) — ISBN
978-1-4222-8817-7 (ebook) 1. Chronically-ill children—Juvenile literature. I. Title.
  RJ380.L533 2014
  618.92'044—dc23
                              2014010626

Picture credits: Artville: p. 104; Corbis: pp. 17, 32; Digital Vision: p. 60; Eyewire: pp.
102, 103, 113, 114; Farina3000 - Fotolia.com: p. 72; Image Source: pp. 34, 49, 69, 116,
119; Life Art: pp. 19, 20, 21, 36, 37, 38, 46, 56, 70, 71, 117, 118; Photo Alto: pp. 87,
101; PhotoDisc: pp. 22, 25, 47, 48, 51, 57, 58, 67, 68, 74, 88, 97, 115; Photo Spin: p.
98; Research Foundation/Camp Abilities: p. 99; The Seeing Eye: p. 86; Susquehanna
Service Dogs: pp. 83, 84, 86.

Contents

KEY ICONS TO LOOK FOR:

 Text-Dependent Questions: These questions send the reader back to the text for more careful attention to the evidence presented there.

 Words to Understand: These words with their easy-to-understand definitions will increase the reader's understanding of the text, while building vocabulary skills.

 Series Glossary of Key Terms: This back-of-the book glossary contains terminology used throughout this series. Words found here increase the reader's ability to read and comprehend higher-level books and articles in this field.

 Research Projects: Readers are pointed toward areas of further inquiry connected to each chapter. Suggestions are provided for projects that encourage deeper research and analysis.

 Sidebars: This boxed material within the main text allows readers to build knowledge, gain insights, explore possibilities, and broaden their perspectives by weaving together additional information to provide realistic and holistic perspectives.

A child with special needs is not defined by his disability.
It is just one part of who he is.

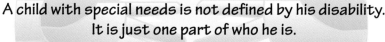

INTRODUCTION

Each child is unique and wonderful. And some children have differences we call special needs. Special needs can mean many things. Sometimes children will learn differently, or hear with an aid, or read with Braille. A young person may have a hard time communicating or paying attention. A child can be born with a special need, or acquire it by an accident or through a health condition. Sometimes a child will be developing in a typical manner and then become delayed in that development. But whatever problems a child may have with her learning, emotions, behavior, or physical body, she is always a person first. She is not defined by her disability; instead, the disability is just one part of who she is.

Inclusion means that young people with and without special needs are together in the same settings. They learn together in school; they play together in their communities; they all have the same opportunities to belong. Children learn so much from each other. A child with a hearing impairment, for example, can teach another child a new way to communicate using sign language. Someone else who has a physical disability affecting his legs can show his friends how to play wheelchair basketball. Children with and without special needs can teach each other how to appreciate and celebrate their differences. They can also help each other discover how people are more alike than they are different. Understanding and appreciating how we all have similar needs helps us learn empathy and sensitivity.

In this series, you will read about young people with special needs from the unique perspectives of children and adolescents who are experiencing the disability firsthand. Of course, not all children with a particular disability are the same as the characters in the stories. But the stories demonstrate at an emotional level how a special need impacts a child, his family, and his friends. The factual material in each chapter will expand your horizons by adding to your knowledge about a particular disability. The series as a whole will help you understand differences better and appreciate how they make us all stronger and better.

—*Cindy Croft*
Educational Consultant

YOUTH WITH SPECIAL NEEDS provides a unique forum for demystifying a wide variety of childhood medical and developmental disabilities. Written to captivate an adolescent audience, the books bring to life the challenges and triumphs experienced by children with common chronic conditions such as hearing loss, mental retardation, physical differences, and speech difficulties. The topics are addressed frankly through a blend of fiction and fact. Students and teachers alike can move beyond the information provided by accessing the resources offered at the end of each text.

This series is particularly important today as the number of children with special needs is on the rise. Over the last two decades, advances in pediatric medical techniques have allowed children who have chronic illnesses and disabilities to live longer, more functional lives. As a result, these children represent an increasingly visible part of North American population in all aspects of daily life. Students are exposed to peers with special needs in their classrooms, through extracurricular activities, and in the community. Often, young people have misperceptions and unanswered questions about a child's disabilities—and more important, his or her *abilities*. Many times, there is no vehicle for talking about these complex issues in a comfortable manner.

This series provides basic information that will leave readers with a deeper understanding of each condition, along with an awareness of some of the associated emotional impacts on affected children, their families, and their peers. It will also encourage further conversation about these issues. Most important, the series promotes a greater comfort for its readers as they live, play, and work side by side with these individuals who have medical and developmental differences—youth with special needs.

—Dr. Lisa Albers, Dr. Carolyn Bridgemohan, Dr. Laurie Glader
Medical Consultants

Health is the first of all liberties.
—Henri Amiel

Words to Understand

aromatherapy: A technique of using different scents to create an effect on the body, such as inducing a certain mood or relaxation.

ibuprofen: A combination painkiller and anti-inflammatory drug. It is often sold under the brand names Advil® and Motrin®.

debilitating: Causing a reduction in one's abilities.

fatal: Causing death.

fatigue: Overwhelming physical and/or mental exhaustion.

residual: Left over, remaining, or secondary. Not primary.

1

AWAKE

The soft scent of spring rose up from the gently swishing grasses. Stretched low so his belly nearly brushed the ground, Rupert loped through the open field. His heart pounded out the rhythm of his steps, sending blood roaring through his body, pulsing in every vein, enlivening each muscle as it rippled with energy and power. He gripped the dirt with his paws and threw it behind him, feeling his muscles working in mighty bursts, sending the plain rolling out beneath him as he ran. The grasses stung his face with their sharp edges and whistled in his ears, urging him forward, whispering for him to run faster, faster through the limitless expanse of open field.

The warm sun sliced through the window and melted across Kayla's bed. Rupert's sleek body slowed. He looked around the bright meadow and sniffed the yellow air. His tongue lolled in a happy pant and he turned to look at Kayla, beckoning her to follow. She wanted to run as well, but the picture faded as the morning sun filled Kayla's sleepy eyes. Coaxed awake by the gently spreading heat, Kayla lay motionless beneath her colorful patchwork quilt and prayed for another hour of sleep. This was the best part of the day, because for a few moments Kayla could lie in perfect comfort, saturated by the sun's early rays, suspended somewhere between asleep and awake.

The last of Kayla's dream spun away as the sound of squeaking faucets and gurgling water rushed into her ears. She listened to the water churning against the porcelain basin, and a wave of sadness broke into her consciousness and drowned her dozing. As she waited to be roused from bed, she listened to her mother running hot bath water. Across the room, the clock's red letters showed 7 A.M. School didn't start until nine, but Kayla had to get up early because it always took her a long time to get ready.

Slowly and reluctantly, Kayla rolled onto her side. The constant ache stretched through her body. Heavy with exhaustion and pain, Kayla inched across the warm sheets. She felt as if someone had poured liquid metal into her body during the night—metal that had settled dense and cold in her bones. By now, it was a familiar feeling.

"Bath's ready," Kayla's mother called, her too-chipper voice echoing off the bathroom tiles. "Better hurry or you'll be late."

Kayla rolled her eyes, but made no answer. Gripping the bedpost with a white-knuckled hand, she shimmied her legs to the edge of the bed and peaked through the sunny window. Rupert sat chained to his doghouse, peering expectantly up at Kayla's bedroom. His tail wagged, and she wondered if he had seen her. "Poor Rupert," Kayla thought. "I bet you had the same dream I had." She returned her attention to her legs and let them flop over the side of the bed. Her feet hit the floor with a thud that sent little daggers of pain reverberating up her shins to her knees. Kayla sucked in her breath.

"Are you up?" her mother questioned, high-heeled footsteps clicking up the hall toward Kayla's room.

Kayla released her pent-up breath in an exasperated burst. "I'm up!" The footsteps paused then retreated back down the hall. Kayla closed her eyes, pulled herself up to standing, and began the long journey to the bathroom.

The cold, slow pilgrimage from warm bed to steaming bath was always the hardest part of her day. Inching along with shuffling feet and hunched back, Kayla looked much older than her fifteen years. She teetered dangerously through the open space, one hand outstretched for balance, one shoulder sliding along the wall for support. By the time she got to the bathroom door, she was already exhausted.

In the bathroom, the air hung moist and thick with fog. Kayla slid her toe through the waiting bath to check the water temperature (nice and hot), then lowered herself into the tub. The water rose around her and enveloped her in its warmth. She pictured the imaginary metal in her bones softening, and her muscles began to relax. These baths were Kayla's morning ritual, a way to wash away the pain and stiffness that had gathered in her body overnight.

As the pain drained from her body and mind, Kayla began taking note of other things. An oil slick covered the surface of the water in a rainbow of tiny bubbles, and a flowery scent assaulted her nostrils. Kayla wrinkled her nose. Her mother was always experimenting with new relaxation and pain-reduction techniques. This week it was **aromatherapy** and bath oils. Kayla sighed. She knew her mother meant well, and everything certainly smelled nice, but it was going to take a lot more than oil and water to fix what was causing her pain.

Kayla's joints felt looser and her muscles more supple after her bath. Moving faster now, she dressed in the black pants and blue sweater her mother had set out on the rocking chair. Normally, she would have hated having her mother pick out her clothes, but in the last few months it had become something of a relief. Kayla had to admit that, though her mom had funny ideas about some things, she did have good fashion sense. Even better, she always picked clothing that was comfortable to wear and free of the little buttons that made Kayla's stiff fingers fumble. When every step of the morning was a struggle, Kayla didn't want to worry about what to wear or how to put it on.

Kayla rubbed the fog from the mirror and leaned toward the glass to inspect her reflection. Although she fully expected it, her heart still sank to see that the rash was still there, running across the bridge of her nose and spreading like huge butterfly wings across her cheeks. She reached for the tubes of makeup sitting before her on the counter. It was special makeup, thick and opaque, the type that actors and models used to cover things like scars and tattoos. Kayla's mother had ordered it through the mail. It was supposed to cover up the rash, but no matter how hard she tried, Kayla couldn't get the makeup to look natural. It was always uneven and pasty, and by the end of the day it became dry and cracked. By the time she got home from school, the makeup looked like a parched desert landscape spread across her skin.

Kayla's hand paused and hovered above the makeup tubes. *Is it better to have a rash or to have makeup caked on like a clown?* she pondered. Her hand passed over the tubes to the **ibuprofen** her mother had left on the counter. While Kayla swallowed the four pills (twice as much as she was supposed to take), she considered going without the makeup for the day. *Maybe it would be a freeing feeling,* she thought, *to not hide behind a mask.* Then she thought about Jackie and Bryn, the beautifully evil twins who roamed the ninth-grade hallways as if they were queens. Like spiders in webs glistening with morning dew, they reeled admirers in with the sparkle of their perfect skin and the silkiness of their blonde hair. They were as snotty as they were beautiful, yet everyone, even the senior girls, seemed to adore them, vie for their attention, and give them anything they asked for. Kayla reached for the dreaded cosmetics. *Beauty must give you some sort of supernatural power,* Kayla thought bitterly and spread the thick makeup across her red, puckered face. She inspected the cream and powder masquerading as unblemished skin. Not very believable, she admitted, but there was no time now for her to do anything but go to school.

Kayla creaked her way down the stairs and into the kitchen. Her mother's briefcase was already gone. Her little brother Brian sat shoveling oatmeal into his mouth, while her father read the newspaper beside him.

"You look nice this morning," her father offered as Kayla searched the refrigerator for something to eat. She shrugged but did not lift her head from the refrigerator doorway.

"I heard a boy on the bus say Kayla looks like a toad," Brian whispered to his father. Kayla rattled the juice bottle in the refrigerator door and pretended not to hear. Her father whispered urgently behind the rustling newspaper. Head down, Brian returned to his oatmeal. His spoon clicked loudly in the uncomfortable pause.

"Are you walking Rupert today?" Her father was obviously looking for something to say.

"Nooo," Kayla drew the word out harshly and set the juice down hard on the table, causing milk to slop over the edge of Brian's bowl and coffee to spill out of her father's cup. What a stupid question to ask. She hadn't been able to walk Rupert for weeks. Quickly realizing his mistake, Kayla's father shifted uncomfortably in his chair. While her father suffered half-hidden by his newspaper, Kayla poured a glass of juice and inwardly scolded herself for overreacting. "Maybe this weekend when there's more time," she added in a gentler tone of voice.

The yellow school bus squeaked to a halt outside the house. Brian grabbed his bag and bolted for the door, but Kayla hung back, waiting for her dad to lift her bookbag onto her shoulders. Then, with her back creaking and groaning under the weight of the bag, she slowly followed her brother out the door and limped toward the bus. As Kayla inched her way down the cracked sidewalk, she tried not to see the impatient faces looking down at her from the bus windows. Instead, she looked at Rupert.

The pepper-colored dog lay in the dust surrounding his doghouse. His head lifted expectantly when he saw Kayla, and his tail began a hopeful wag. Kayla quickly looked away, but it was too late. Rupert was on his feet and tugging against his chain. Lifting a paw toward her and cocking his head to one side, he whined, then yelped as he strained against his collar. Not wanting to encourage him or give him false hope, Kayla pretended not to notice his excitement. But Rupert wasn't so easily put off. He made two gymnast leaps into the air, then rolled his head from side to side, trying to wiggle out of the restrictive collar. When that didn't work, he dug his feet into the dirt and leaned backward against the chain. His muscles popped with strain, but it was no use. He was stuck.

Sorry, Rupert, Kayla thought. *No walks today.* As if he had read her mind, Rupert sat resignedly in the dust and watched as Kayla's father gave her a boost onto the high steps of the bus. Kayla stumbled clumsily down the narrow passageway of knees and feet, sucked in her breath as she passed the snickering twin evils, and collapsed in her seat.

Dreading the day, Kayla pressed her face against the window. Little puffs of fog rose around her nose and mouth. As the driver put the ancient vehicle into gear, Kayla caught a glimpse of Rupert through the fogging glass. From her high seat, Rupert looked small and forlorn as he sat chained to his doghouse, and Kayla felt a wave of pity. *Don't worry Rupert,* she thought as the bus pulled away, *I know just how you feel.*

WHAT IS CHRONIC ILLNESS?

The word *chronic* means "lasting a long time or frequently recurring." A chronic illness is a long-term illness or an illness that comes back over and over again. In most cases, the symptoms of a chronic illness can be treated, but the illness itself cannot be cured. For example, allergies can be a form of chronic illness. Let's say that you have an allergy to cats. A doctor can give you different types of medicines to treat symptoms like a runny nose and itchy eyes, but the doctor cannot make you stop being allergic to cats.

A person can be born with a chronic illness or can develop one later in life. Sometimes a person will grow out of a chronic illness as she gets older. This usually only happens

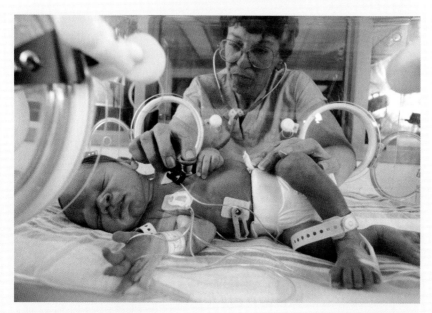

A baby who is born prematurely is at risk of developing some form of chronic illness.

Make Connections:
Who Gets Chronic Illness and Why?

 People of all ages, cultures, and backgrounds can develop chronic illnesses. Such illnesses occur for many different reasons. Some of these reasons are genetic, meaning that the illness or the potential to develop the illness runs in the family. Some causes of chronic illness are environmental, related to something the person comes in contact with (foods, chemicals, pollutants, stressful situations, or other outside factors). In many cases, doctors cannot find one reason for a person's chronic illness. Not everyone who has a genetic predisposition toward a chronic illness develops that illness. For example, perhaps both your mother and brother have allergies, but you do not. On the other hand, some people develop chronic illnesses even when no one else in their family has a history of that illness. Doctors believe that chronic illnesses usually develop from a complicated mix of both genetic and environmental factors.

with young people. For example, a child with allergies may no longer have allergies as an adult. Occasionally, a chronic illness in an adult might go away as mysteriously as it began. However, in many cases, once a person develops a chronic illness, she will have that illness for the rest of her life. Some chronic illnesses can be mild. Others have symptoms that are **debilitating** and difficult to control. Still other chronic illnesses can be **fatal**.

A peak flow meter measures the lung capacity of a child with asthma.

Asthma Phases

Clinical Signs

	Normal	Mild	Moderate	Severe
Respiratory Rate		↑	↑↑	↑↑↑ or 0
Breath Sounds		Wheezing	Unequal	Decreasing or Absent
Use of Accessory Muscles			↑	↑↑

Arterial Blood Gas Changes

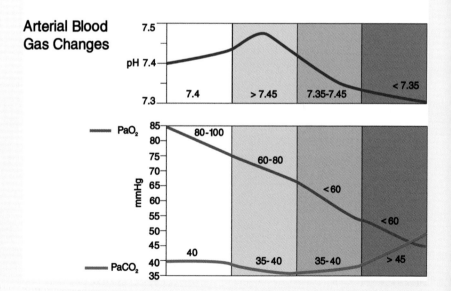

	Normal	Mild	Moderate	Severe
pH	7.4	> 7.45	7.35-7.45	< 7.35
PaO₂	80-100	60-80	< 60	< 60
PaCO₂	40	35-40	35-40	> 45

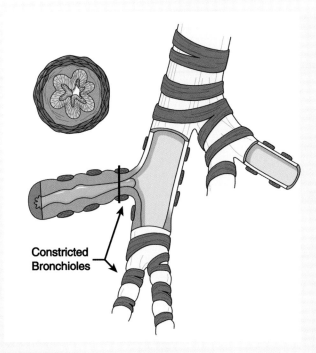

Asthma is a chronic illness caused by constriction of the tubes inside the lungs.

TYPES OF CHRONIC ILLNESSES

There are many different types of chronic illnesses, and the symptoms of these illnesses vary widely. Some chronic illnesses, like allergies, asthma, and migraine headaches, are quite common. You probably know people who have these conditions or may even have one yourself. Some other chronic illnesses that you may be familiar with are heart disease, which causes hardening of the blood vessels and arteries in the heart and can lead to heart attacks; diabetes, a disease characterized by not being able to use food appropriately for energy; arthritis, which is characterized by pain and swelling in a person's joints; and cancer, a disease in

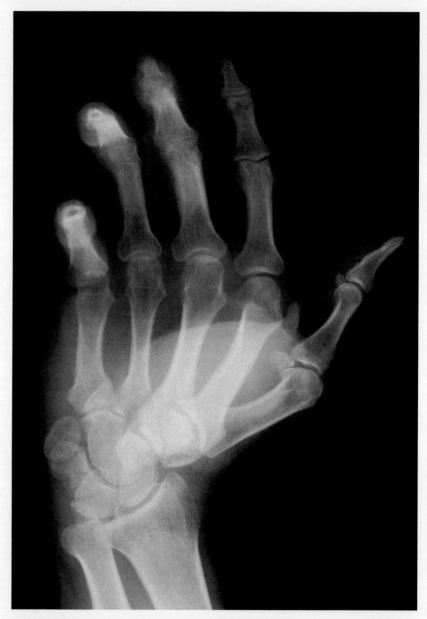

Arthritis can cause chronic pain in the joints of the hands.

which certain cells begin to grow and multiply out of control, invading and taking over other cells and tissues. Some chronic illnesses begin in childhood, while others occur more commonly in older patients. Some chronic illnesses that you may not have heard of include lupus, epilepsy, multiple sclerosis, and chronic **fatigue** syndrome. You will learn more about these and other chronic illnesses in the following chapters. Though some of the specific illnesses we will discuss are relatively rare, chronic illnesses as a whole are very common. Chances are, you know someone who lives with a chronic illness. Though we do not yet know what specific chronic illness Kayla has, we can see that one of her symptoms is pain. Chronic pain—pain that recurs frequently and often does not respond to treatment—is one type of chronic medical condition that many people suffer with.

CHRONIC PAIN

Chronic pain can occur for many different reasons. For example, it can be a symptom of another chronic illness, the **residual** effect of an injury sustained long ago, or it can be a chronic condition all on its own with no apparent or identifiable cause. Probably the biggest challenge facing people who suffer from chronic pain is learning how to live a full and happy life when every day brings intense physical discomfort.

Chronic pain occurs more often among older people than among young people.

Chronic Back Pain

Some of the most common things that contribute to back pain are back injuries, obesity (the stress of carrying large amounts of excess weight can cause pain in the back), mental and emotional stress (which can cause tensing of the back and shoulder muscles), and bad posture.

Research Project

Use the library and Internet to find out more about pain caused by a person's nervous system. Choose three conditions caused by nerve pain to research further. What causes each condition? What are its symptoms? How is each condition treated? What challenges do people face who have each of these conditions?

Chronic Joint Pain

Pain in the joints, such as the pain that results from arthritis, often occurs when years of use begin to cause damage to the delicate cartilage and soft tissues in the joints. Chronic joint pain is most common among elderly people, but it is also common among athletes who may damage their joints through years of strenuous exercise and physical competitions. Many women have also experienced chronic pain in their feet, ankles, knees, hips, and backs after years of wearing high-heeled shoes.

Headaches

Many people experience recurring and debilitating headaches. On the one hand, headaches may be the result of such things as another medical disorder, stress, or sensitivities to certain foods. On the other hand, a person's recurring headaches may have no discernible cause at all.

Text-Dependent Questions

1. Explain what makes an illness "chronic." What are three examples of chronic illnesses?
2. What is one of Kayla's symptoms?
3. How might high-heeled shoes be connected to chronic pain?

Pain in the Nervous System

Some recurring pain has its roots in the nervous system (the system that carries messages between the brain and the body). The nervous system is responsible for relaying the message of pain to the brain. For example, if you burn your finger, pain receptors in your finger send a message through the nervous system to your brain and your brain registers the message as pain. However, some people experience chronic pain when their nervous system sends pain messages to the brain even when there is no pain stimulus. This may be the result of an old injury, another medical condition, or may occur for no apparent reason.

Pain is part of being alive.
—Harold Kushner

Words to Understand

stroke: A sudden blockage or rupture that causes a loss of blood to the brain resulting in temporarily or permanently impaired movement or function; can cause death.

catalyst: A trigger. Something that sets other events in motion.

dermatologist: A doctor who specializes in treating diseases and disorders of the skin.

side effect: Something that is secondary to or accompanies the primary positive effect for which medication is prescribed. Side effects are usually mild and tolerated by patients, but sometimes side effects can be so severe that they warrant discontinuation of the medication.

2

WHEN IT ALL BEGAN

It had all started two years ago with a terrible sunburn. Kayla had taken Brian to the community swimming pool for the day. Like she had promised her mom, every hour Kayla made Brian get out of the pool and dry off so she could douse his squirming body with sunscreen. Each time, Brian protested loudly, then screamed that Kayla had gotten the sunscreen in his eyes.

"Shut up and let me put this on you, or you'll have skin cancer when you're fifty," Kayla warned. Instead of scaring him into submission, however, her words just made him scream louder. But as soon as he was back in the water, splashing the other kids and scrambling for his turn on the slide, he seemed to forget the apparent horrors of sunscreen.

Kayla, though charged with sunscreen duty, was not going to let anything so silly as possible skin cancer when she was fifty get in the way of a perfect tan. The winter had dragged on forever, and then the spring had been rainy and cold. The weather these past months left Kayla feeling weak, cranky, and depressed. The day was finally hot and sunny, the first really good swimming day of the summer, and she was ready to enjoy it. Since Kayla had recently turned thirteen, her mom had even let her wear a two-piece swimsuit for the first time (twin evil and twin eviler had been wearing two-piece swimsuits since they were five years old and had already graduated to bikinis), and she was not going to waste the opportunity. Donning headphones to block out the screaming kids and dark sunglasses to block out the world, Kayla spread her beach towel on the deck's prickly concrete and settled in to become a sun goddess.

The shrill lifeguard's whistle pierced Kayla's eardrums. Her eyes popped open and her head shot up. Where was Brian? How long had she been asleep? The whistle signaled the end of the swimming day, and children bubbled over the side of the pool like a mass of ants out of a hill. But Brian wasn't with them. Panic nipped at Kayla's stomach. She stood up slowly and felt dizziness swirl her vision. Blinking, she peered through the waves of heat rising off the concrete and scanned the perimeter of the chain link fence. Not finding Brian there, she headed for the shade of the cinderblock shower building. The world spun around her as she walked.

The fear rising in Kayla's throat kept her from noticing how her skin stretched like dry leather as she walked. At the entrance to the boy's changing rooms, she leaned into the cool, dark doorway and called Brian's name. A hollow echo of her voice reverberated between the damp walls.

"Here I am!" Brian's happy shout rose behind her. Kayla spun around in a rush of relief. Brian clutched a soda in one hand and his beach towel in the other. His eyes widened as he gazed at his older sister. "You're red." His pronouncement was solemn.

Now that her fear was gone, Kayla began to realize how much her skin hurt and how dry her throat felt. She hadn't had anything to drink all day, and now she felt like she was about to be sick.

"Give me a sip." She reached toward Brian's soda. Brian took a careful step back and cradled the half-empty bottle to his chest.

"Clara bought it for me," he proclaimed in response to his sister's demand. Kayla's fear of moments ago quickly turned to annoyance. Brian continued to waver while Kayla's impatience grew.

"What, is Clara your girlfriend now?" Kayla asked, knowing her little brother would cringe at the idea. Brian looked at the soda and his nose wrinkled.

"Noooo." He looked at his sister then back to the soda, his expression showing doubt. "She just bought it for me." He looked deep in thought. With an unhappy pout, he finally offered the bottle to his sister. She took a gulp. The sticky sweetness made her gag. "Are you going to have cancer when you're fifty?" Brian asked. Kayla rolled her eyes and took another swig from the bottle. Brian watched her and shifted his weight from foot to foot. "Well, are you?"

"Don't be an idiot." Kayla tried to smile as she said it, but it came out sounding cruel. The truth was that she felt in no mood for Brian's questions. Brian looked hurt for a moment, and then he switched to a more aggressive stance.

"You're mean," he retorted.

"Well you're stupid," Kayla fired in return. Brian opened his mouth to say something, but then snapped it shut, reached up, and pinched Kayla's red arm instead. Kayla yowled in pain. Seeing that she was temporarily impaired, Brian grabbed the soda bottle from Kayla's hand.

"I'm going to tell Mom you drank all my soda," he complained, trying to press Kayla further.

Kayla felt like she was going to faint; she knew she didn't have the energy to fight with him. Instead, she bent painfully and pulled a dollar from her bag. "Here. Buy some candy, and we'll go home."

He took the money and trotted happily toward the vending machines.

That evening, between lying with ice packs pressed to her skin and running to the bathroom to throw up, Kayla inspected her blistering arms and legs. She called it a sunburn, but really it was like a scorching, red furnace had spread its fire across her body. It was certainly not the first time she'd ever been sick, or even the first time she'd been badly sunburned, but it marked the last time she ever felt well.

Kayla spent the rest of her summer vacation paying for that sunburn. Every time she went out into the sun she got a rash, and every time she was out in the heat she felt sick. She had to sit in the shade of the shower building when she took Brian to the pool, and she rarely had the energy to play volleyball at the park. Even walking Rupert became more of a punishment than a pleasure.

Although Kayla always walked him, Rupert was actually the neighbor's dog. Mrs. Pennelly had never liked dogs, but she seemed to keep Rupert out of some misguided feeling of obligation to her dead husband. Kayla hadn't even known the Pennellys had a dog until Mr. Pennelly died. The day after the funeral, Mrs. Pennelly led Rupert out of the house and chained him to a tree. It made everyone sad to look at Rupert. After all, it seemed like it would be better to give Rupert away than to keep him chained outside the way she did, but no one was going to tell Mrs. Pennelly that. She might be old, but she didn't seem like the type of person who welcomed advice from anyone. She seemed more like the type of person who chased little kids out of her yard with a broom.

But then Mrs. Pennelly had a **stroke**, and things started to change. Partially paralyzed on one side, she had a hard time getting around and began relying on other people to help her with things like grocery shopping, cooking, cutting the lawn, and cleaning her house. Kayla's mom joined with some other ladies who took turns bringing dinner to Mrs. Pennelly, and Kayla's dad started mowing Mrs. Pennelly's lawn. One day while cutting the grass, he suggested to Kayla that she take Rupert for a walk.

"Shouldn't we ask Mrs. Pennelly first?" she questioned her father as visions of the crooked old lady coming after her with a broom flared in her head. But her dad had said no, that Mrs. Pennelly preferred not to be bothered, and Kayla took Rupert for their first walk. That weekend Kayla and her dad built a doghouse for Rupert. Kayla and Rupert had been taking daily walks ever since.

Before the sunburn incident, Kayla had spent many afternoons throwing a Frisbee to Rupert in the park. The summer of the sunburn, however, Kayla could only walk Rupert in the mornings before the sun got too high or else she'd break out in a rash. And she noticed other disturbing things as well, things that had nothing to do with her sunburn. By the end of their walks, Kayla's knees and hips ached. If Rupert pulled her along too fast, her chest began feeling tight and sore.

Their walks were getting shorter, and Kayla started taking naps as soon as they got home. Kayla's dad scolded her for shortening Rupert's walks. After all, it was the only time the animal got to leave his doghouse. Kayla's mom said summer was making Kayla lazy. Kayla would have almost welcomed this explanation, but deep down she knew something far more serious than summer laziness was going on.

Each day her certainty grew. Something was frighteningly wrong with her, but she had no idea what it was.

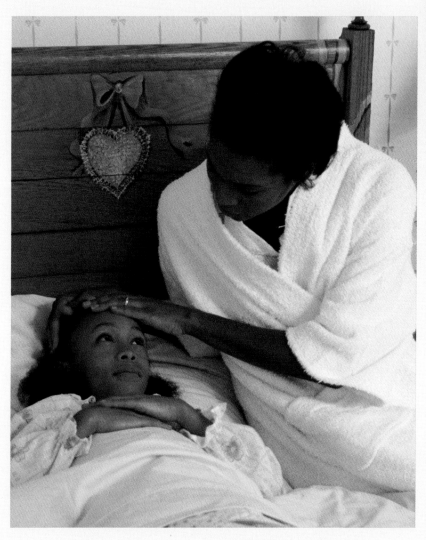

Children are not immune to chronic illness.

THE ONSET OF CHRONIC ILLNESS

Kayla associates her terrible sunburn with the onset of her feeling sick. Many people with chronic illness can identify a specific event that correlates with the onset of their symptoms—a time before which they felt well and after which they never felt well again. For many people this might be a bad illness, a serious accident, or a stressful event. For example, many women with chronic illness pinpoint pregnancy or giving birth as the **catalyst** for their condition. Other people can remember their illnesses starting after an event like a car accident or serious injury. Highly emotional and stressful life events, like the death of a loved one, are also often cited as the beginnings to chronic illnesses.

Although people relate events like these to the onsets of their chronic illnesses, the event they describe is not the *direct* cause of their illness. For example, when a woman recalls pregnancy as the beginning of her illness, it does not usually mean that being pregnant gave her the illness. Rather, events like those mentioned above are oftentimes characterized by many changes in a person's body. If a person already has a genetic predisposition toward developing a certain chronic illness, an extremely physically or emotionally stressful event could trigger that genetic potential and lead to an illness.

Although some people can pinpoint a time when their chronic symptoms seemed to begin, other people may not know when or how their symptoms started. Even though Kayla sees her sunburn as the time when she stopped feeling well, she also mentions that she had felt tired and depressed for months before she got her sunburn. For many people, the onset of symptoms of chronic illness is slow and vague. In the beginning of a chronic illness, symptoms are often general and difficult to identify. The person usually does not yet realize that they are sick. Instead, the person

A child with a chronic illness needs love and support from her parents.

Make Connections: The Need for Support

 Although Kayla is experiencing symptoms of chronic illness for the first time, her next-door neighbor Mrs. Pennelly has been struggling with long-term health problems for years. After her stroke, she needs members of the community to help her with daily activities like cooking, cleaning, and cutting the lawn. The need for family and/or community support is a common situation for people with chronic illnesses, who may find their ability to perform daily tasks impaired.

may notice feeling tired, achy, and depressed, but assume that these feelings are caused by ordinary events like being overworked, not getting enough sleep, or the weather. For many people, the most identifiable symptom they have of the early stages of a chronic illness is simply the lingering, nagging feeling that something is wrong.

TYPES OF CHRONIC ILLNESS: SKIN ILLNESSES

At the beginning of Kayla's chronic illness, she did not know that anything more than a bad sunburn was wrong. However, even after her sunburn healed, skin problems continued. Skin disorders like rashes can be either symptoms of other chronic illnesses or chronic illnesses on their own.

Vitiligo

Chronic skin illnesses and conditions can have many different causes. Vitiligo appears on the skin, but it is actually a disorder of the immune system. In fact, it is an autoimmune

disorder, meaning that it is a disorder in which a person's immune system begins to attack her own body. The immune
system is supposed to recognize foreign or dangerous invaders in our bodies and destroy those agents before they
can do serious harm, while leaving our own healthy cells in-
tact. The immune system of a person with vitiligo, however,
recognizes the person's own pigment cells (the cells that
give our skin, hair, and eyes their color) as foreign invaders.
Her immune system attacks and kills these pigment cells,
leaving white or colorless patches in the person's skin and

*Sometimes a bad sunburn can be associated with the begin-
ning of a more serious illness.*

hair. Vitiligo is genetic, and though it may have a strong effect on the way a person looks, it does not threaten her overall physical health.

A skin condition can be especially embarrassing for an adolescent.

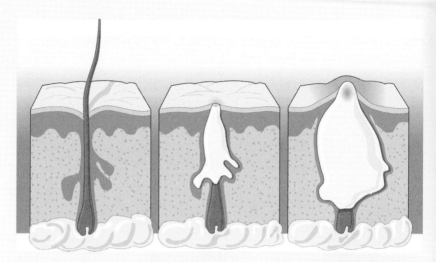

Acne is caused by pores that become clogged and infected.

Acne

Many people have acne, especially when they are young, but some people have acne that is so severe and long lasting that it could be called a chronic skin illness or condition. Acne can result from a number of different causes. It can be a bacterial infection on the skin, in which case a **dermatologist** may be able to provide medicine to kill the infection.

Research Project

Find out more about one of the skin conditions described in this chapter. Use the Internet to locate any recent discoveries or treatment options that have been made for this condition. If no new developments have occurred, describe one research study that investigated this condition and list any conclusions the study reached.

Sometimes acne is the result of food or skin allergies, and changes in diet or environment can relieve the symptoms. Acne also commonly results from hormonal imbalances in a person's body. Doctors can often prescribe medication to help a person with this type of acne as well. On the other hand, acne is sometimes caused by certain medications. Corticosteroids are medications that are often used to treat chronic illnesses involving muscle inflammation and immune system functioning. Corticosteroids, however, may cause acne. Thus, a person taking corticosteroids for the treatment of one chronic illness may find that another chronic condition develops as a **side effect** of their treatment.

Eczema

Often called dermatitis, eczema is a name given to a group of very common skin disorders involving the repeated appearance of dry, itchy rashes. The rashes often feel hot and may in severe cases become raw and bleed. People with eczema are believed to have a genetic tendency to be extremely sensitive to skin allergens that would not have an effect on other people's skin. Eczema can occur alone, or it can be part of another chronic illness or group of allergies. Dermatologists can offer many treatments for eczema, but like other chronic illnesses, there is no cure.

Text-Dependent Questions

1. What is vitiligo? What causes it and what does it look like?
2. List three possible causes of acne.
3. What is eczema's main symptom?

Illness changes us.
—Louis E. Bisch

Words to Understand

hormones: Body chemicals that stimulate other organs and tissues to behave in specific ways.

anemia: The medical condition of having low levels of iron in the blood. This condition can cause excessive tiredness because blood cells use iron to carry oxygen around the body.

inconclusive: Does not yield enough evidence to warrant a conclusion or determination.

3

THE VISIT

Kayla shivered in the thin gown. The paper beneath her bare legs crackled as she shifted her weight on the narrow table. The harsh light glinted off the metal instruments on the counter and gave the jar of cotton balls an unnaturally white glare. Sitting on too-small chairs across from her, Kayla's parents looked equally uncomfortable in the sterile examining room.

As that sunburn summer had slipped away and a new school year had begun, Kayla felt no better than she had in the previous months. Her frequent skin rashes continued to appear, and exhaustion came and went like storms through her body. Even when the fatigue passed, rivulets of pain remained, trickling through her veins, appearing first in her arms, then stabbing unexpectedly in her legs, then whispering their way to her chest. This fleeting pain seemed to always be on the move, gnawing in one location and then migrating to another part of Kayla's body, remaining out of reach and one step ahead of her ability to predict it.

That fall, it seemed like Kayla's mom never stopped talking about menstrual periods and changes and the power of **hormones**. Kayla wished that her mom was right, that everything she was experiencing could be chalked up to "becoming a woman." In fact, she had started getting her period only a couple months ago, and she certainly felt cranky and achy when she had it. But she couldn't quite believe that her mother was right. After all, Evil-dee and Evil-dum had also gotten their periods, and they seemed happier and

sickeningly sweeter than ever before. They certainly weren't breaking out in rashes or acting tired and achy all the time.

As fall progressed and Kayla's exhaustion and aches worsened,
her parents decided it was time to see a doctor.

When the doctor entered, he seemed as cold and sterile as the
room itself. He asked for a description of her symptoms, and Kayla
described the terrible sunburn of earlier in the summer and the
rashes and exhaustion that followed. "Sounds like you had a little
bit of sunstroke," the doctor replied.

His comment seemed somewhat condescending, and Kayla began to feel silly as she continued her story. She tried to explain how
the rashes kept reappearing long after the sunburn was gone and
how she started feeling pain in her chest and cold in her joints. The
more she spoke, the more stupid she thought she sounded. After all,
how could a sunburn make your chest and bones hurt? As she
spoke, Kayla caught a glimpse of her parents. Their restless shifting
made them look as if they were also pondering this question.

When Kayla finished telling the doctor about her symptoms, he
asked to see her rashes. Kayla swallowed a sinking feeling as she
lifted her sleeves to show her arms, for she knew there was nothing
there to see. She shrugged. "I don't have any today," she mumbled.

The doctor spent the remainder of their visit asking questions
about Kayla's schoolwork, activities, and social life. He wanted to
know if she liked school, how her grades were, and if she had many
friends. He addressed a few of his questions to Kayla, but mostly he
just looked at her parents. Kayla felt self-conscious as her parents related how her grades were falling and how she had quit the volleyball team. Her face burned when her mother shared Kayla's special
hate for the popular Jackie and Bryn. *I can't even get away from the
twin evils in the doctor's office*, Kayla thought bitterly. The doctor
raised an eyebrow in her direction, and Kayla wondered briefly if
she had made that comment aloud.

When he finally gave his opinion on Kayla's medical condition,
the doctor barely looked at Kayla. There was no doubt, he told
them, that Kayla had been sick at the beginning of the summer and

probably should have seen a doctor then. "Sunstroke is a serious thing, and it shouldn't be taken lightly." Kayla watched her parents shrink with guilt and felt a twinge of anger.

"At the moment, however," the doctor continued, "there aren't any *visible* signs that Kayla is sick." He emphasized the word "visible," and Kayla thought again about her mysteriously disappearing rash. "I'm going to order some blood work to check for things like **anemia**." Kayla cringed at the thought of needles.

"Now, I know it may be difficult to hear," the doctor started carefully in a softer tone of voice. He was changing gears, and Kayla's interest was suddenly piqued again. "But I think, in light of what you've told me about Kayla's academic and social struggles"— Kayla winced at the doctor's choice of words—"perhaps we need to consider the possibility that Kayla may be malingering." The doctor paused for a reaction. Kayla's parents were giving each other a look, but Kayla didn't know what the look meant. The air in the little room suddenly felt heavy with seriousness.

What's malingering? she wondered desperately, but everyone seemed involved in such sober thought that she couldn't bring herself to ask. Whatever it was, it sounded horrible, like something that would eat at your flesh until you were just skin and bones, making you cough and wheeze until you wasted away and died. Malingering, malingering—the word rolled around in her head, conjuring up visions of her funeral. There was something absurdly pleasurable about the thought of lying tragically in a casket surrounded by flowers and weeping mourners.

The doctor's words broke through her thoughts "I realize this may seem implausible, but it's really very common among children Kayla's age, especially with all of the physical and emotional changes they are experiencing."

Kayla thought about what the doctor said. If it was common, then it didn't seem like she was going to die from it. But then again, if malingering was so common, why hadn't she ever heard about it? And why on earth wasn't anyone explaining what they were talking about to her? She watched her parents shake hands with the doctor.

She guessed she'd just have to wait for them to explain things to her when they got home.

By the time they had walked to the lab and she had her blood drawn, Kayla was exhausted. She desperately wanted to know what the doctor had meant, but her parents were strangely silent, and she suddenly felt afraid to ask. Sitting in the back of the car, Kayla waited anxiously for some revealing conversation to begin in the front seat, but before her parents could say anything that would give her a clue, she found herself drifting to sleep.

When they returned home from the doctor on that day two years ago, Kayla noticed that her parents' mood had suddenly changed. Her mother had reached into the back seat of the car, gently shook Kayla awake, and asked with a smile, "What would you like for dinner, Honey? We'll make anything you want."

Kayla felt sick and tired and only shrugged. Encouraged, however, by her mother's smile, she asked the question that had burned in her at the doctor's office. "What's malingering?"

Kayla's mother and father shared that look of theirs, but did not immediately answer Kayla's question. After a pause, Kayla's mother spoke carefully. "It's nothing to be afraid of, Kayla," her mother said in a reassuring tone of voice. "Your dad and I are going to make a nice dinner, and then we're all going to sit down together and talk about it after supper."

Despite her mother's tone of voice, Kayla was not at all reassured. Why wouldn't anyone tell her what was going on? Her mother and father never cooked dinner together. Kayla knew it was just an excuse for them to lock themselves away so they could talk about her without her around.

That evening, as the sounds of muffled voices, clinking silverware, and sizzling food wafted up to her, Kayla opened the family's dictionary on her bedroom floor. Her heart beat rapidly as she flipped the thin pages to "m" and slid her finger down to "malingering."

Tears caught in Kayla's throat as she read the definition: "exaggerating, feigning, or drawing out an illness in order to avoid work, duties, or obligations."

Kayla could not believe the words she had read. Faking it! After all these months of feeling sick and tired, of having rashes and pains, that stupid doctor thought she was faking it! She recalled the doctor's visit, his condescending tone, the look he'd given when she told him she didn't have a rash today, the way he'd ignored her as he spoke to her parents, the way her parents looked at each other when the doctor said the word "malingering." Her parents believed it too! For a moment, Kayla's heart filled with a heavy mix of embarrassment and rage. But then, an even worse feeling crept into the back of her mind: doubt.

Kayla thought about how she always felt the worst in the mornings—right before she had to go to school. She considered how her rashes mysteriously disappeared. She contemplated how impossible it seemed that a sunburn could have caused all these symptoms. For the first time a terrible thought occurred to her. It was a thought that would plague her for the next year.

Maybe she had been faking it all along. Or worse yet, maybe she was crazy, and maybe there was nothing wrong with her but her head.

THE DIFFICULTIES OF DIAGNOSIS

One of the most difficult roadblocks that people with chronic illnesses face is the difficulty of diagnosis. Because the symptoms of many chronic illnesses are unpredictable or **inconclusive**, diagnosis for these disorders can be frustratingly elusive. Family members and doctors may become suspicious of the person's symptoms and suggest that the person is malingering, not really sick, or imagining their illness. When faced with the doubt of others, individuals with chronic illnesses often begin to doubt themselves. They may try to downplay or ignore their symptoms in order to avoid ridicule, tell themselves that symptoms like tiredness and pain are normal, or even begin to fear that they are "going crazy."

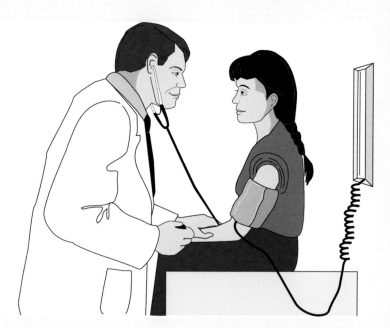

Diagnosis of a chronic illness is often a long process.

The results of a blood test can indicate a chronic illness.

Many people with chronic illness (or their parents) spend a number of years seeking a diagnosis. Many chronic illnesses share similar symptoms—especially symptoms like general tiredness and achiness. During this time, a person with a chronic illness may receive a number of incorrect diagnoses as doctors work to pinpoint the exact cause of the person's symptoms.

A correct diagnosis is important not only so a patient may begin proper treatment but also so that the patient can understand what he is going through. A correct diagnosis helps the patient mentally as well as physically by showing him why he is experiencing symptoms in addition to how he might control these symptoms. Until a person finds a diagnosis for his illness, he cannot begin to fully cope emotionally or physically with his symptoms. For many people, the pre-diagnosis period of chronic illness is a time

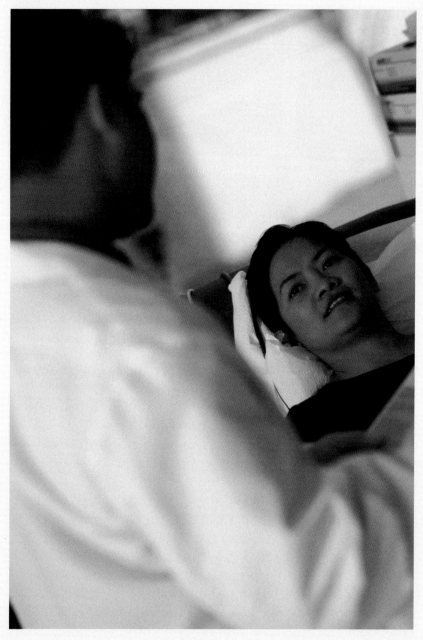

Chronic fatigue syndrome is not easily diagnosed.

marked by feelings of fear, self-doubt, embarrassment, and powerlessness.

TYPES OF CHRONIC ILLNESS: CHRONIC FATIGUE SYNDROME

Feelings of fatigue are common symptoms of many chronic illnesses. However, in chronic fatigue syndrome, incapacitating fatigue of the body and the mind is the patient's major symptom. This condition is a little understood but increasingly common chronic illness. According to some estimates, approximately one million people suffer from this chronic condition.

A person with chronic fatigue syndrome feels tiredness so severe that it interferes with even the most basic daily tasks like getting out of bed in the morning and thinking clearly. A person with chronic fatigue syndrome often has a general feeling of illness as well, making the person feel like he constantly has the flu. Different body systems and organs are also often affected. For example, the person may begin

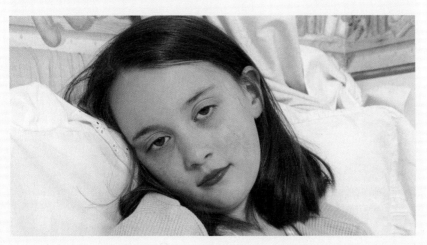

A person with chronic fatigue syndrome is constantly tired.

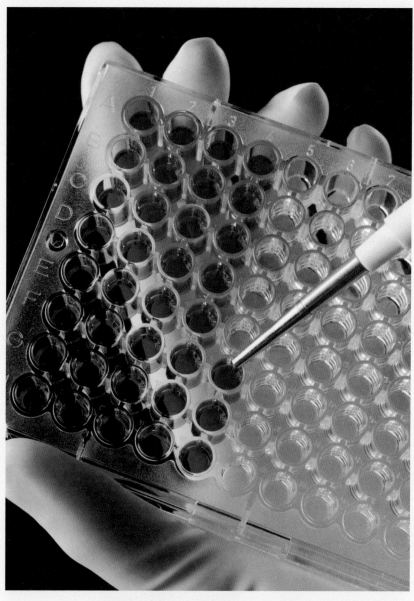

Researchers have not yet found a medication to treat chronic fatigue syndrome.

Research Project

Read about someone who has chronic fatigue syndrome in a book, magazine, or on the Internet. Describe what this person experienced before he or she was diagnosed. Has this person's life changed since finding out what is wrong? What challenges does this person face? How has he or she come to terms with chronic fatigue syndrome?

to have intestinal difficulties or blurred vision. Muscle pain throughout the body is another common symptom of the syndrome.

Currently, no one understands the cause or causes of chronic fatigue syndrome, though doctors suspect it has to do with a combination of genetic and environmental factors. Just as there is no clear understanding of the causes of chronic fatigue syndrome, there is also no one treatment for the disorder. Treatment plans usually focus on a combination of medication, supportive therapy (such as psychological counseling or attending a support group), and lifestyle changes (like reducing stress, increasing exercise, and eating healthfully).

Text-Dependent Questions

1. Kayla's doctor suspects that she may be malingering. What does this word mean? Why does her doctor reach this conclusion? How does Kayla feel about it?
2. What is chronic fatigue syndrome?

Health . . . is the first and greatest of all blessings.
—Lord Chesterfield

Words to Understand

inflammation: Pain, redness, and swelling in body tissues, usually as the result of infection or injury.

4

DENIAL

After the doctor's appointment, Kayla denied her illness to everyone, including herself. She blamed her frequent rashes on acne and her tiredness on being lazy. If her joints ached, she told herself not to be a wimp; if she woke in the morning feeling unable to walk Rupert, the word "malingering" echoed in her brain, forcing her to get dressed and grab Rupert's leash.

Kayla's parents seemed to accept her act willingly, even thankfully. They had asked so many questions of Kayla after the doctor's visit—questions about her feelings toward them, about her friends, about her happiness. Suddenly they were more worried about her mental state than her physical symptoms. Kayla hated being under the microscope this way, and her parents seemed to hate it as well. When Kayla decided to behave as if everything were normal, her parents seemed eager to join the charade.

Despite Kayla's success in convincing herself and her parents that she was healthy again, the effort it took to deny her illness was almost more exhausting than the sickness itself. Every night when Kayla went to bed, she felt thankful that she'd made it through the day and fearful that she might not make it through the next one. She felt like she was losing pieces of herself little bits at a time, as though every day that passed ate away another part of her. But still she pushed on, refusing to believe that she was truly sick and refusing to let others see her struggle lest they think she was faking it.

Months passed. The school year wore on, and by early spring it seemed like everyone had almost forgotten that she had ever appeared to be sick.

A day came, however, when Kayla and her family could no longer deny that something was terribly wrong. Kayla had woken up feeling particularly bad. When she looked in the mirror that morning, she gasped. A large, purplish rash had spread over the bridge of her nose and across both of her cheeks. It looked like a huge, horrible butterfly had landed on her face and imprinted its open wings below her eyes. As she gasped, pain ricocheted through her lungs and bounced against her rib cage, making her double over in agonized surprise. Despite the undeniable rash and pain, Kayla whispered "malingering, malingering" to herself, eased Rupert's leash off the nail in the hallway, and slipped past her parents and out the door.

It had been an unseasonably cold day. The sky was dark and an icy drizzle seeped from the clouds. Rupert shivered beside her and periodically shook the rain from his black and white fur. He had been reluctant to come out of his doghouse that morning, but Kayla whispered "malingering" to herself and coaxed Rupert forward by waving his Frisbee.

They never got to play Frisbee that day. They hadn't gone far when the pains in Kayla's chest suddenly sharpened and her legs went rubbery. Rupert looked alarmed when Kayla stopped unexpectedly in the middle of the sidewalk. He began to whine as her hand went to her chest and she gasped for breath. Head cocked to one side, Rupert studied Kayla, his whining growing more urgent. Kayla felt like her ribs were collapsing into her lungs, and she coughed painfully.

Rupert pulled against the leash, and Kayla stumbled forward, exhaustion and pain seizing her body and blinding her. She felt the ground shift from sidewalk to grass beneath her feet, and she placed her hand against the rough bark of a tree. Rupert had the hem of Kayla's jacket in his mouth, and as he pulled, she sank to the ground.

Enveloped by pain and fear, Kayla barely noticed how Rupert

sped off barking down the street. She knew she wasn't far from her house, but she didn't know how she could possibly get home again. The light drizzle turned to rain, and cold seeped through Kayla's skin as she began to cry. Then, through tears mixing with the cool rainwater, she saw Rupert running back down the street with both her parents behind him.

As her parents knelt beside her, the pain in Kayla's body drowned out all other thoughts and sounds. The strangest feeling came over her. The world tilted, and Kayla became detached and far away. She could see her parents talking, her mother grasping desperately at her jacket, her father stooping to shield her from the rain, Rupert standing quietly behind them, watching everything closely. But the whole scene seemed slow and warped, like music underwater. Watching from her skewed perspective, everything suddenly struck her as being very funny—the way her crisply proper mother was kneeling in her nightgown in the rain, how Rupert had torn down the street like Lassie to go get help, how the water looked like tears streaming down her fathers face, and funniest of all, how she had insisted on behaving as if she were healthy, and here she was lying beneath a tree in a cold downpour. A car splashed past on the street, and Kayla saw its taillights go red as the brakes squeaked and the car shifted into reverse. She opened her mouth to laugh, but a dagger of pain stuck her throat.

The world tilted again and the slow, faraway picture rushed back down the tunnel of Kayla's vision. Kayla gasped as the scene shifted back to normal and she found herself once again wet and in pain beneath the tree. She felt her father lifting her from the ground and carrying her toward the parked car, but all she could do was whisper, "Why don't you believe me?" and then simply, "I'm sick," over and over again.

THE PROBLEM WITH DENIAL

Denial is a common stage in many illnesses. Kayla experiences two types of denial—the denial of others and the denial within herself. There are many reasons why people deny their illnesses. A person may not want to appear sick because they don't want people to give them special treatment or think about them differently than they did before the illness. Thus, individuals may deny to others that they have an illness. On the other hand, a person beginning to experience a chronic illness may deny the illness to herself. It is often hard for a person to accept that she is sick because accepting illness also means accepting that her life may

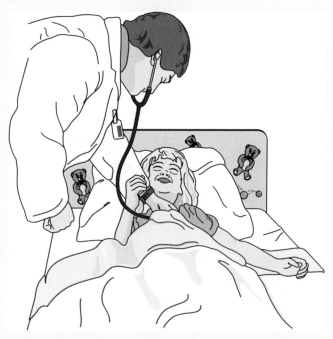

Chronic illness cannot be treated until it has been faced and accepted.

Research Project

 Find out more about denial, using the Internet and the library. Why do psychologists believe that people experience denial when facing an illness? Does denial play a role in other life traumas, such as dealing with the death of a loved one? Have you experienced denial in your life? Apply what you have learned about denial to your own situation. Do you understand yourself better now? Do you think it will be easier for you to avoid denial in the future—or do you think that denial is unavoidable? Explain your answer in terms of the role psychologists believe denial plays in mental health.

have to change. She may no longer be able to do the things she once did easily, or it may take more effort to do these things. It can be hard to realize one's limitations or to gather the extra strength to move beyond those limitations. Most people with a chronic illness will go through a stage when they deny the illness or the seriousness of their symptoms. Some people may live with denial for many years, even after receiving a diagnosis for their illness.

Families and loved ones of people with chronic illnesses may join in the denial as well. Kayla's parents would never intentionally endanger their daughter's health. Nevertheless, they are quick to believe Kayla when she behaves as if she is no longer sick. People never want to see someone they love become sick or limited by an illness. The desire to see their loved one healthy, maintain a normal lifestyle, and preserve their daily comfort and happiness may lead a family to unknowingly join in the cycle of denial.

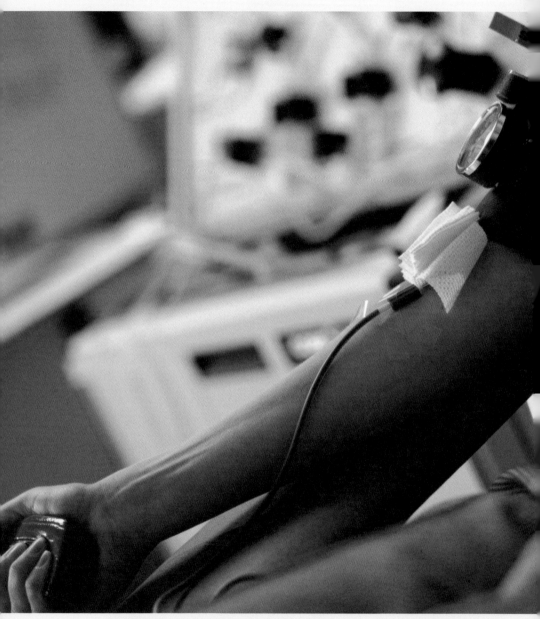

The tubes and equipment associated with illness may be
frightening, both to the patient and to family and friends.

Denial can be dangerous for a number of reasons. If a person denies her illness, she will not seek appropriate treatment for her condition. She may push herself to do things that she should not, or may refuse to recognize her body's warning signs indicating that she is pushing herself too hard. When a person with a chronic illness is in denial, she increases the chances of harming herself or allowing her illness to get worse. When a person or family falls too deeply into the trap of denial, it may take a frightening event like the one Kayla's family experienced to make them see the reality of the illness again.

TYPES OF CHRONIC ILLNESSES: DIVERTICULITIS

Diverticulitis, another chronic illness, is a condition of the intestines in which enlarged pockets form in the intestinal lining. Food and other particles can get trapped in these pockets. This then causes **inflammation**, infection, and severe abdominal pain.

Diverticulitis and other similar chronic illnesses of the gastrointestinal tract are extremely common among people over

Make Connections

Doctors believe that eating a diet rich in fiber while you are young may prevent the development of uncomfortable intestinal disorders when you are older. High-fiber foods included vegetables, fruit, and whole grains.

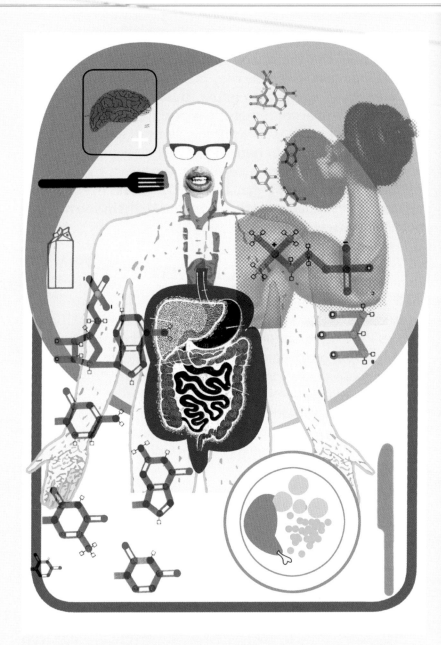

Diet, mental condition, exercise, and many other factors all play a role in good health.

Text-Dependent Questions

1. Explain how denial played a role in Kayla's life in two different ways.
2. What causes diverticulitis?

the age of forty. Many doctors believe that these illnesses of the digestive system are largely caused by years of eating a diet low in fiber. Once a person has a condition like diverticulitis, her doctor may recommend a special low-fiber diet to give her digestive system time to rest and heal. She may also need to take antibiotics.

As she starts to feel better, her doctor will have her gradually add foods with fiber back into her diet. Some doctors believe now that eating a high-fiber diet may prevent flareups in people who have diverticulitis.

Health is not valued until sickness comes.
—Thomas Fuller

Words to Understand

autoimmune: Having to do with antibodies that attack an organism's own body cells.

legitimate: Having a good reason. Based on reality or logical reasoning.

unfounded: Lacking legitimacy, evidence, or reason.

anti-inflammatories: Medications that counteract inflammation in the body.

corticosteroids: A class of medicine that fights inflammation.

5

DIAGNOSIS

Mike, the young intern working in the emergency room that morning, was the one who first suspected that Kayla had lupus. Days later, after the diagnosis had been confirmed, he explained to Kayla that it was her butterfly-shaped rash that had tipped him off. "A classic symptom of lupus," he had called it. Mike said lupus was a chronic **autoimmune** disorder. "A little," he said, "like having your body be allergic to itself."

Kayla thought about this as she touched her face in embarrassment, trying to hide the red lumps from the cute, young doctor.

She loved how everyone at the hospital treated her like an adult. After a certain set of blood tests, Mike had even sat down with Kayla and explained what all the numbers meant. She didn't understand a lot of it, but Mike said the most important thing the tests showed was the existence of auto-antibodies—antibodies that Kayla's immune system had made to specifically target her own healthy cells. Mike told Kayla that her case was pretty serious, because the lupus had caused inflammation around her heart and lungs. Nevertheless, Mike was so calm and matter-of-fact when he spoke that Kayla never felt frightened by what he told her. Kayla even told Mike about how all her symptoms had started after her bad sunburn, and to her delight, Mike said he was not at all surprised to hear it. He said that bad sunburns could sometimes cause small changes in the DNA in a person's skin cells. If a person had lupus, their immune system could get confused and begin attacking their skin cells, causing rashes.

While Kayla felt relieved to know she hadn't been malingering after all, the diagnosis of lupus seemed to immerse her parents in fear. They walked gingerly around her hospital room and spoke in quiet tones. One day, at the end of visiting hours, Kayla's father lingered after her mother and Brian headed to the car. Kayla watched her father clasping and unclasping his hands. He cleared his throat twice before speaking.

"I've been taking Rupert for his walks this past week," he said haltingly. He didn't look at Kayla as he spoke. Kayla smiled, but sensed she shouldn't say anything. "You know," her father continued, "I was actually going to ask Mrs. Pennelly if you could have Rupert for your birthday . . . but the old lady doesn't seem to want to give up her dog."

"That's okay, Dad," Kayla replied, but inside she was disappointed. Getting Rupert would have been a nice way to make up for having spent her fourteenth birthday in the hospital.

"Anyway," her father continued, looking more uncomfortable than ever, "I just want you to know, Kayla, that your mom and I feel really terrible about what happened. . . . You know, it wasn't that we didn't believe you were sick," he said, suddenly speaking quickly, his face twisting with guilt. "We just didn't know what to believe, and when you started seeming better . . . well . . . we just wanted you to be better."

Kayla wasn't sure, but she thought her father was crying, and the thought was horrifying to her. She wanted to stop him, to tell him that everything was fine, that she had been angry before but that she wasn't angry now. Before she could say anything, however, he continued. "We're going to make it up to you, Kayla. Your mother and I, and your brother too, are going to do everything we can to get you well." He leaned forward to give his daughter a hug.

Kayla wanted to say something but couldn't think what, and her father was already on his way out the door. As he passed over the threshold, he turned back toward Kayla's bed. "You're going to be okay," he stated before leaving the room. Kayla knew he had meant the statement to be reassuring, but deep down, she thought he sounded frightened.

When Kayla thought about it, she figured she should probably be frightened as well after receiving a diagnosis like lupus. But instead of being frightened, she actually felt profoundly relieved. Knowing that she really was sick and that people really did believe her was like having a great weight lifted off of her shoulders. When it came time for Kayla to leave the hospital, she was actually disappointed to be going.

The greatest part of her stay at the hospital was right at the end when Mike, the doctor who had helped her so much, took Kayla to the Teens Talk meeting. Teens Talk was a group of people who were all Kayla's age and who were all living with chronic illnesses. Her first Teens Talk meeting was a really eye-opening experience. Some of the participants were staying at the hospital. Kayla could tell because they wore hospital bracelets, had IVs in their arms, or were wheeled into the meeting in their hospital beds. Looking at some of the other participants, however, Kayla would never have guessed that they were sick.

She was the newest member of the group, and everyone welcomed her. They told her she could say anything she wanted about her illness and could ask anything that came to mind, but if she didn't feel like talking yet, that was okay too. For the first time, Kayla did feel like talking about her illness, but she wasn't sure what to say, so she spent most of the meeting listening to what everyone else had to say. After the meeting, Mike escorted Kayla back to her room, where she pondered this new group to which she suddenly belonged. These were people who would understand her, she realized, who had gone through what she was going through, who could give her advice. She wished the group met more than once a month.

Mike had warned Kayla that there would be big adjustments waiting for her back at home. He told her she would have to start taking medications every day and get used to frequent visits to the doctor. He said some of her medications would have side effects and that she would have to work harder than most people to make sure she stayed healthy. This meant eating right, keeping her sensitive skin out of the sun, and avoiding undue stress as much as possible.

At first, Kayla didn't take what Mike was telling her too seriously, but he warned her that things would be different when she was no longer in the hospital setting where there were so many people to support her. Kayla thought about this and soon realized that Mike was right. Not everyone was like the people she'd met at Teens Talk. Most of the people her age didn't know anything about chronic illness.

She would have to return to school with this rash on her face. The evil twins were sure to say something about it, and everyone knew she had been in the hospital. What were they going to think of her when she told them that she had lupus? How was she going to be able to have fun if she was always worrying about her health and if she felt sick all the time? Worst of all, she had asked Mike if the medicines were going to make her lupus go away. A grave look came over his face when she asked this question.

"I'm sorry, Kayla," he had responded, "But there is no cure for lupus." He paused for a moment to let the news sink in and then continued more brightly. "But we are going to work very hard to find the best possible treatment for your symptoms, and with a little luck and a lot of determination, you're going to be able to live comfortably and happily and keep your lupus under control."

Mike spoke confidently. Kayla longed to believe him, but deep down she wasn't so sure.

REACTIONS TO DIAGNOSIS

When receiving a diagnosis of a chronic illness, people are likely to react to the diagnosis in very different ways. These reactions may include fear, guilt, relief, and confusion. People with chronic illness—as well as their family and friends—may have all, some, or none of these feelings before, during, and after they learn of a diagnosis.

Fear

Fear is, of course, one of the first and most common reactions to learning that one has any illness. A person may fear that she will no longer be able to do the things she loves, that people will treat her differently, that a diagnosis of illness means she will feel sick forever, or even that she may

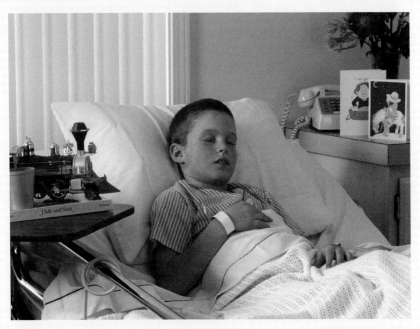

Being sick can be frightening, especially for children.

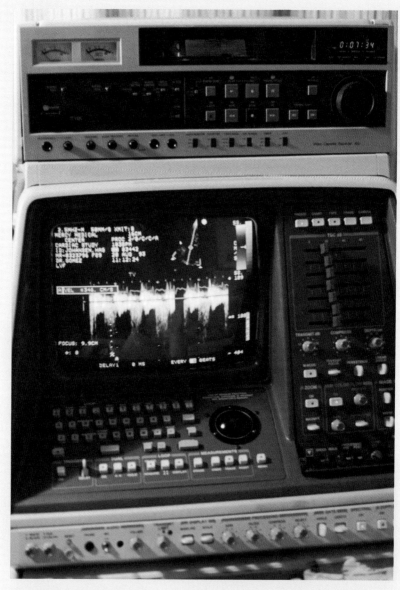

A variety of equipment may be used to monitor the body functions of someone with a chronic illness. When the purpose of this technology is not understood, patients and family may find the lines and beeps frightening.

die. Some of the fears a person may have will be **legitimate**, but others will be **unfounded**. The best way to deal with fear is through education. The more a person learns about her illness, the fewer unfounded fears she will have. Education will also teach the person how to deal with her legitimate fears, treat her illness appropriately, and minimize the health risks that her illness poses.

Guilt

One of the first reactions Kayla's parents have to her diagnosis is guilt. They feel guilty that they did not believe Kayla when she said she was sick and that they did not recognize the signs of her illness before. Guilt is a very common feeling experienced both by the loved ones of people with chronic

Parents may feel guilty that they did not recognize a child's chronic illness earlier.

illness and by the people with chronic illnesses themselves. Family members may feel guilty that they did not do more to help their loved ones. Individuals with chronic illness may feel guilty because they believe that they somehow caused their illness, perhaps by leading an unhealthy lifestyle or failing to recognize that they were sick. Guilt is a common and natural emotion, but it can be destructive if it continues for too long. If the individual's or family's guilt remains unresolved, they may wish to speak with a health professional, therapist, counselor, or other supportive individual about their feelings.

Family members may initially dismiss chronic headaches as unimportant.

Relief

One of Kayla's first reactions to her diagnosis of chronic illness is relief. This may seem surprising or even strange, but it is actually quite common. People with chronic illnesses often spend so many years suffering from symptoms, self-doubt, and the skepticism of others that when they eventually receive a diagnosis, they feel relieved to finally have a name for what they are experiencing. They may also feel relieved to know they are not alone; others have faced similar experiences.

Confusion

After initial reactions like fear, guilt, and relief, confusion may set in. The newly diagnosed patient may feel confused about her illness and what it will mean for her future. Many chronic illnesses have multiple and complicated treatment options, and the patient may feel confusion about how to choose a treatment plan. After being diagnosed with a chronic illness, many people will turn to their local libraries and to the Internet to gather as much information about their illness as they can. They may feel overwhelmed by the amount of information and feel dazed by conflicting theories. Speaking with health-care professionals, getting information from national or scientifically recognized organizations, or speaking with other people who have the same illness can help a person during this time of confusion.

THE IMPORTANCE OF SUPPORT GROUPS

Shortly after being diagnosed with lupus, Kayla joined a support group called Teens Talk. Support groups often play an important role in the lives of people with chronic illnesses. In support groups, individuals can find communities of people who understand their struggles, fears, desires, and tri-

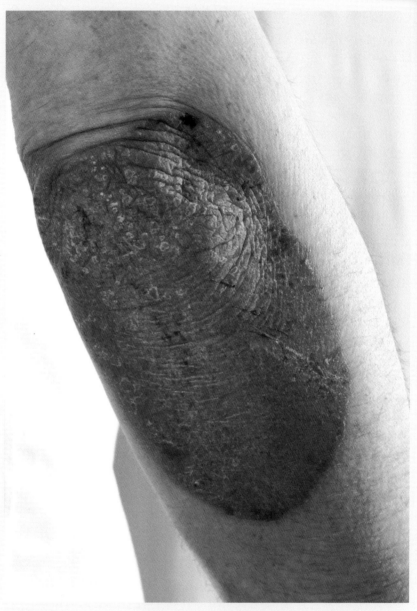

Psoriasis is painful skin condition. Like lupus, it is caused by an immune system disorder.

Make Connections: Lupus

After being sick for a year, Kayla is finally diagnosed as having lupus (Systemic Lupus Erythematosis), a chronic autoimmune disorder. Autoimmune disorders are disorders in which a person's immune system, the system that protects us from sickness and disease, attacks her own body. Having lupus is like having your body be allergic to itself. Instead of only attacking harmful invaders, your immune system begins killing your own healthy cells.

Some of the most common symptoms of lupus are inflammation and pain in one's joints, chronic fever, fatigue, skin rashes, and kidney problems. A butterfly-shaped rash across a person's cheeks and nose is a very identifiable sign of lupus. Not all lupus patients have this rash, but when this rash is seen in combination with other symptoms, it may help doctors to identify the person's illness. Some people have mild forms of lupus, which are relatively easy to control. In these forms of lupus, the immune system may attack the joints and skin, but not any vital organs. Other people have very serious forms of lupus in which their immune system begins to attack vital organs like the heart, kidneys, and lungs. Kidney failure is also a common result of lupus and something that lupus patients and their doctors must work carefully to prevent.

Different types of medications may be used in the treatment of lupus. The most common are nonsteroidal anti-inflammatories (NSAIDs) like aspirin and ibuprofen. Treatment with corticosteroids is also quite common, but these drugs can have unpleasant side effects like weight gain, a round face, acne, easy bruising, and thinning of one's bones.

Lupus is only one of many different types of autoimmune disorders. It is estimated that between 500,000 and 1.5 million people in the United States have lupus. It is most common in women, and is usually first diagnosed in young women who have reached the age of childbearing.

Text-Dependent Questions

1. Why are support groups helpful to people with chronic illness.
2. What is an autoimmune disorder?

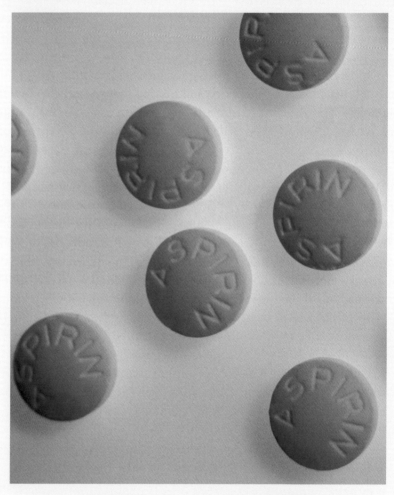

Aspirin may be used to treat lupus.

Research Project

There are many kinds of support groups out there. Use the Internet to locate support groups in your area. Make a list of each group and what its purpose is. Are there support groups in your area intended specifically for young people?

umphs. Support groups can provide a positive atmosphere for discussing the many issues that come along with chronic illness. People with chronic illnesses can find out about support groups in their area through their doctors, hospitals, community organizations, libraries, and on the Internet.

You will never really understand a person . . .
until you climb into his skin and walk around in it.
—Harper Lee

Words to Understand

seizure: A sudden attack where the central nervous system's electrical rhythms are disturbed, clouding consciousness.

6

MRS. PENNELLY

Back home, life was different and strange. Kayla's father had taken time off work, and her mother came home early every day. Each meal was suddenly a carefully planned, well-balanced affair, and medical books littered the surfaces in every room. Brian wavered between creeping quietly around the house when discussions about Kayla's illness were going on and throwing loud tantrums when everyone seemed to be ignoring him.

That first week back from the hospital, Kayla also received an explanation for Rupert's Lassie-like behavior on the day she'd collapsed in the rain.

A few days after coming home from the hospital, Kayla limped her way outside to say hello to Rupert. The faithful dog sat as he always did, beating his tail in the dirt as Kayla approached. Today, however, instead of untying Rupert for their walk, she sat in the dirt beside him and ran her hand between his floppy ears. He licked Kayla's nose and lay down contentedly beside her.

As Kayla stroked Rupert's fur, Mrs. Pennelly's screen door swung open. Kayla heard the uneven "tha-thump" as Mrs. Pennelly carefully made her way down the front steps. Kayla's heart beat faster. She hadn't spoken with the elderly woman since she'd had her stroke, and now Mrs. Pennelly's drooping face and sagging body made Kayla feel awkward. As she watched her neighbor make her lumbering way across the yard, she felt almost scared, as though Mrs. Pennelly were really the witch Kayla had often imagined.

Sharp pangs jabbed Kayla's knees as she struggled to stand, but Mrs. Pennelly waved her good hand at Kayla. Her other arm hung heavily at her side, her body curving toward it as if the dead hand were a weight pulling her to the ground. Kayla thought she should get Mrs. Pennelly a chair, but the old woman placed her hand on Kayla's shoulder instead and made the slow, laborious journey to sitting.

"It's hard for an old lady to get down," she coughed hoarsely as she sank in slow motion. She spoke out of one side of her mouth while her lips drooped on the other side of her face. Her tongue lolled thickly, making her words difficult to understand. Kayla could not tell if Mrs. Pennelly's crooked lips were smiling. "I noticed you haven't been walking Rupert lately," she continued. Kayla opened her mouth to speak, but Mrs. Pennelly shook her tilted head. "Your parents told me what happened."

Kayla did not know what she should say, so she did not say anything at all. The gray-haired woman breathed heavily beside her, and Kayla wondered if that was all she was going to say. After a moment, Rupert stood, crossed over to Mrs. Pennelly's side, and lay down with his head on the old woman's lap. Kayla looked at Rupert's chain lying across her lap and thought how sad it was that Rupert was always chained when he should be free to play and run.

The woman's eyes followed Kayla's gaze. Although her body was crippled with the years, her mind, Kayla realized, didn't seem to have aged.

"You probably think it's horrible that I keep him chained up out here," the old woman said, and Kayla felt even more uncomfortable than she had been a moment ago.

"No, I don't," Kayla began to reply, but the woman's good hand waved to cut off Kayla's statement.

"Yes, you do," Mrs. Pennelly said, "and you're right. It's a horrible, horrible thing to do." The old woman leaned back on her good arm for support and stared at something in front of her. "Rupert is a very special dog."

Kayla looked at Rupert's speckled fur. She certainly liked Rupert, but he didn't look that special.

"He used to be my husband's constant companion," Mrs. Pennelly went on, speaking almost as if Kayla wasn't there. "My husband had epilepsy, you know." Kayla hadn't known that, but Mrs. Pennelly said it more like a statement than a question, so Kayla didn't reply. "I used to take care of him pretty well, but when we got older, we thought it might be good to get a service dog who was trained to help if something happened." She looked down at Rupert. "My husband sure loved this dog."

Kayla had never known much about the Pennellys. Even though they had lived next door her whole life, Kayla found herself wondering about them for the first time. She was suddenly very interested in what Mrs. Pennelly had to say. When the old woman continued, her slurred voice sounded sad.

"It was the strangest thing when we got Rupert. This dog," she said, patting the fur-covered head, "knew that Roger was going to have a **seizure** before it even happened." Mrs. Pennelly sighed. "You'd think it would have made me happy, but it actually made me mad. It was like this dog knew my husband even better than I did. Rupert never left Roger's side, and when Roger was going to have a seizure, Rupert would lead him over to a safe place and make him lie down. He'd lie next to Roger the whole time the seizure was going on. Then, when it was over, he'd run find me or someone else for help."

Kayla wasn't sure she could believe the story Mrs. Pennelly told. She looked at Rupert panting happily with a somewhat vacant look in his eyes. He certainly didn't look like an animal with a sixth sense at the moment, but thinking back to his behavior that day in the rain, Kayla could believe that Rupert might have some special abilities. She wondered if Mrs. Pennelly knew about how Rupert had helped her on their walk that day. She was just about to tell her, when the old woman spoke again.

"Would you believe I spent years being jealous of this dog? Then, when Roger died, I just didn't know what to do with him." Kayla noticed that Mrs. Pennelly didn't refer to Rupert by his name. "I couldn't stand to get rid of him because he reminded me of Roger, but I couldn't stand looking at him for the same reason. So I just brought him outside and tied him to that tree."

Kayla thought for the first time how sad Mrs. Pennelly must be, alone in her house, unable to get around like she used to because of her stroke, reminded of her dead husband every time she saw her dog. Kayla wanted to say something to let Mrs. Pennelly know she understood, but she couldn't think of a single thing to say.

As if she had read Kayla's mind, Mrs. Pennelly reached over and patted her knee. "You know, your dad came over here and asked if I would give Rupert to you." Mrs. Pennelly's watery voice slowed, then caught in her throat. "I'm very sorry that you're feeling sick, Kayla. You can walk Rupert whenever you feel able, but I just don't think I'm ready to give him up."

Kayla couldn't tell if Mrs. Pennelly was crying, but she felt pretty sure that she might cry herself. "That's okay, Mrs. Pennelly," she managed to choke, "I understand."

The two women sat in silence for a moment. Mrs. Pennelly grasped Kayla's hand, then gently released it. "Now, why don't you go get your dad so he can help this old lady out of the dirt." This time, Kayla was sure that Mrs. Pennelly had smiled as she spoke. Kayla smiled too. Feeling somehow lighter than she had before, she struggled to her feet and went to get her father.

After that, Kayla spent a lot of time with Mrs. Pennelly. She found Mrs. Pennelly surprisingly helpful and understanding for an old person. It was strange, but Kayla felt closer to her elderly neighbor than she felt to anyone her own age, with the exception of the people at Teens Talk. But she only got to see them once a month, and if Kayla wanted, she could talk to Mrs. Pennelly every day. After school, Kayla often limped directly over to Mrs. Pennelly's house, where the unlikely pair first complained about their aches and pains, then laughed at how funny they must seem.

In addition to having had a stroke, Mrs. Pennelly had also suffered from arthritis for years, and she was able to give Kayla lots of tips for easing her aching muscles. She was the one who told Kayla to start every morning off with a hot bath, and Kayla was pleased with how much better she always felt after the morning soak.

Mrs. Pennelly wasn't just helpful when it came to talking about being sick, however. She had great advice about a lot of things and had a sense of humor as well. As Kayla watched the old woman moving slowly around the kitchen, she wondered how she ever could have envisioned her brandishing a broom. Kayla talked to Mrs. Pennelly about how much she missed playing volleyball—and about her love/hate relationship with the beauty-twins, Jackie and Bryn. When she told Mrs. Pennelly about her nicknames for them, Evil-dee and Evil-dum, the elderly woman laughed so hard Kayla thought she might fall down. When Mrs. Pennelly finally stopped laughing, she moaned, "Ohhh, that made my bones hurt," and wiped a bit of spit from the crooked side of her mouth. Then she nodded her head understandingly when Kayla confided that, even though she couldn't stand them, she couldn't help but envy the evil twins as well.

Mrs. Pennelly was also the one who first suggested that Kayla's family develop Brian Time. With Kayla being sick, much of the family's time focused on her and her illness. It seemed as though her parents were forever driving Kayla to doctors' appointments, reading about treatments for lupus, or asking about how she was feeling and what they could do to make her feel better. With all of this constant attention, her little brother Brian quickly began to feel left out. Kayla hadn't really noticed this at first, but one day Mrs. Pennelly asked how Kayla's illness was affecting Brian. It hadn't really

Research Project

Find out more about service dogs, using the Internet. Describe the different ways dogs can help people with various physical challenges. How are these dogs trained? How can people volunteer to help train dogs for people with special needs? Is this something you would be interested in doing? Why or why not?

occurred to Kayla that Brian might be affected by her illness at all. But once Mrs. Pennelly asked, Kayla realized that sometimes whole days went by when no one seemed to hear from Brian.

To deal with this problem, Mrs. Pennelly suggested the invention of Brian Time—time each day devoted to Brian alone, when he got to be the focus of attention and when Kayla's illness was guaranteed *not* to be discussed. Kayla found that Brian Time turned out to be good for the entire family, for it was the one time each day when everything felt normal again, when the talk wasn't just about illness, and when they could all forget for a few moments that Kayla was sick.

Make Connections: Service Dogs for People with Special Needs

Most people know about guide dogs that help people who are blind. But did you know that there are also hearing-ear dogs for people who are deaf and service dogs for people with other disabilities? Service dogs allow people with conditions such as blindness, deafness, and physical disabilities to lead more independent lives. Some chronic illnesses can lead to physical disabilities. Service dogs for people with disabilities are trained to retrieve objects that are out of reach, help people in and out of bed, chairs, or wheelchairs, pull wheelchairs around, and run to get help if their person needs assistance.

Service dogs can be helpful companions for people with physical disabilities.

A service dog gives its owner greater freedom and mobility.

SEIZURE DOGS

Rupert was able to help Kayla the day she collapsed in the rain because he had been trained as a service dog. But Rupert also has a special ability. He is able to detect when a person is going to have an epileptic seizure before it occurs. This is a very rare ability that some dogs have been found to possess. When one of these dogs realizes that his person is going to have a seizure, he leads him to a safe place, encourages him to lie down, stays with his person during the seizure, and then goes to find help.

Service dogs often wear special uniforms, like harnesses and orange vests. These uniforms show other people that

Service dogs can go where ordinary dogs would not be allowed.

These puppies will grow up to be Seeing Eye® dogs.

the dog is doing an important job and should be allowed to accompany his person to places where dogs would not normally be allowed to go, such as businesses and public transportation.

THE NEED FOR A NORMAL LIFE

After being diagnosed with lupus, Kayla needs to adjust to a life filled with doctors' appointments and constant discussions of illness. This can be hard for anyone. People in this situation may feel that they no longer have anything in their life that is not about illness. This can be especially difficult for young people who are struggling to form their identities

Children with a chronic illness need to live normal lives despite their disabilities.

and who want to participate in school, extracurricular, and social activities.

The life changes that come with the diagnosis of chronic illness can also be difficult for siblings, especially younger siblings, of people with chronic conditions. With so much of their parents' attention focused on dealing with a newly diagnosed illness, siblings may feel left out. Families in which one child has a chronic illness often benefit from setting aside time that focuses exclusively on the other child or children. Families also benefit from setting aside time for fun activities that the whole family can enjoy—activities that allow everyone to have a mental break from the strain of coping with illness. Even small amounts of time—like a few moments spent reading together, sitting down to watch a television show, or using dinner conversation as an opportunity to talk about other matters—can be helpful in reestablishing the feeling of a normal life.

TYPES OF CHRONIC ILLNESSES: EPILEPSY

The term "epilepsy" is given to chronic seizure disorders. Seizures occur when areas of the brain become overactive, sending out electrical signals to the body that are much stronger than normal. Irregular electrical activity in the brain can happen for many reasons. For example, certain drugs, flashing lights, scar tissue from a head injury, or abnormal growths in the brain can trigger seizure activity. A person is only diagnosed with epilepsy, however, if she experiences repeated seizures for which there is no apparent cause. Some children have seizures associated with fevers but then do not have seizures as they grow older; these children do not have epilepsy. People with epilepsy have seizures that occur whether or not they have fevers, and their seizures continue to occur in adulthood.

Text-Dependent Questions

1. Why do other children in the family have a hard time when a sibling has a chronic illness?
2. What is a seizure? How is having a single seizure different from having epilepsy?
3. How is epilepsy treated?

Epilepsy is usually treated with medication. In many cases, a person's seizures can be completely controlled with medicines. This, however, does not mean that the person has been cured of his condition. If he stops taking his medication, his seizures will likely return. Some people have surgery or special diets to control their seizures. Young people sometimes grow out of epilepsy as they get older, but for many people, epilepsy is a life-long condition.

Death cannot have the final word.
—Ossie Davis

Words to Understand

stereotypes: Oversimplified beliefs or ideas held about a group of people.

7

TRAGEDY

The bus ride to school was the typical horror. Halfway there, Evil-dee turned around in her seat and shouted, "Kayla, what did you do to your makeup?" Kayla could hear Evil-dum snickering beside her. Then the second blonde head whirled around, hair spraying in a golden fan across the aged, green seat. "We can give you some lessons on that if you want."

Her sickeningly sweet tone made Kayla want to vomit all over their pretty little heads. Instead, she pretended that she hadn't heard and kept staring out the window. She would tell Mrs. Pennelly about the incident this evening, and together they'd imagine wonderful ways to get back at the wicked twins—magnificent ways to turn their perfectly blonde hair green or embarrass them horribly in front of all their admirers—things that Kayla could never do, of course, but that were certainly fun to imagine.

When the bus finally pulled in front of the school, Kayla remained in her seat while the rest of the students rose and flooded forward around her. She never joined the jostling, pushing crowd in its crush to escape the dusty-smelling vehicle. Instead, Kayla waited for the danger of leaden feet and smashing elbows to pass before she made her slow way down the empty aisle to where Mr. Tims, the bus driver, waited to help her down the steep steps. By the time she made it off the bus, the sidewalks were deserted; all the other students had already entered the building, leaving only their ringing laughter behind.

While her ninth-grade classmates whooped and shouted on their way to homeroom, Kayla threaded a path toward the gymnasium. By the time she arrived at school, the effects of her morning bath were already wearing off. Kayla started every school day with physical therapy to help keep her muscles loose. During the two years before her diagnosis, Kayla had fallen behind in her schoolwork, especially in math. Now, each morning while her classmates struggled with geometry, Kayla struggled with weights and stretching exercises. Later in the day, when her classmates went to study hall, Kayla attended her own small geometry class with a few other students who needed extra help with math.

When Kayla had first returned to school and learned that her classes were going to be different from everyone else's, she was horrified. Having just been diagnosed with a chronic illness, Kayla wanted to blend in at school as much as possible. Now even her class schedule was going to make her stand out as different.

In total contrast to what Kayla had expected, however, most of her classmates were great about her illness. Far from laughing at her or being awkward around her, they were genuinely curious and wanted to be helpful. Her first week back from the hospital, everyone was asking Kayla questions. One day, her science teacher pulled her aside after class and asked if she'd like to give a report on lupus to help her classmates understand what she was going through. She hadn't felt comfortable talking to her whole class about something that affected her so much, but she thought that at some point in the future, she might like to give such a presentation. The first few weeks after the hospital stay, Jermaine, a boy Kayla had known since elementary school, even offered to carry her books for her. At the end of class, he'd appear at the side of Kayla's desk and sweep her books into his arms before she could even protest.

After a while, the novelty of Kayla's illness began to wear off. People stopped asking questions, and Jermaine stopped his book carrying. But rather than being upset at the loss of the extra attention, Kayla was relieved to be treated like a normal person again. She also knew that Jermaine and many of her other classmates would still help her if she asked, and that knowledge was a great comfort.

Despite the kindness and understanding of so many of her class-mates, Kayla still struggled with her emotions. She was always try-ing to hide her rash-covered face from others and tried desperately to walk without the stoop that announced her pain to the world. On the one hand, she wanted to chat lightheartedly in halls, go out with her friends after school, and make daring plans for the week-ends. On the other hand, she constantly feared that her pain and slowness would make her a drag, so she hung back from the discus-sions of parties and plans to have fun. Usually if someone asked her to go out for some fun, her answer was an automatic no.

Today, however, something was different. The morning had be-gun badly with the usual soreness and the jibe from the twin evils, but by the time her physical therapy was over, Kayla was feeling re-newed and optimistic again. At lunch, she felt contented as conver-sation hummed around her. She smiled when Jermaine approached the table. He sat down beside Kayla and beamed with unusual enthusiasm.

"So, Kayla," he nudged her arm, "you've got to come out with us tonight." It was Friday, and Kayla could tell by the eagerness in Jermaine's voice that he had something planned. "I just got my li-cense, and my parents are letting me take the car." Kayla thought his head was about to explode with pride, and his excitement was con-tagious. Nevertheless, she had a policy of avoiding going out, and though it pained her to do so, she began to shake her head.

Jermaine spoke quickly before she could say the word no. "Oh come on, Kayla." Annoyance streaked his voice. "It's just a movie. You're not that sick."

Kayla's head shot up as if she'd been stung. Her eyes widened in hurt surprise.

Jermaine jumped back in his seat as if he'd also been taken by surprise. His mouth opened, but for a second nothing came out. "Oh geeze . . . I'm . . . I'm sorry, Kayla," he stammered. Kayla wasn't sure whether to be offended or not, but Jermaine apparently didn't want to stick around while she figured it out. "Look," he said as he stood up and gathered his books, "just be ready at seven, and we'll pick you up." Before Kayla even had a chance to protest, he was already walking away.

Kayla couldn't think clearly for the rest of the day. Every time she tried to concentrate, visions popped into her head of sitting in Jermaine's car, driving fast along the highway with the windows down and music blaring. She realized that this might actually be the first time she was going out with friends since she became sick two years ago. Soon, she was as nervous as she was excited.

Mrs. Pennelly had been urging her for months to spend more time with people her own age. She'd be proud to hear that Kayla was taking her advice. (Kayla figured she'd leave out the part about Jermaine not giving her any choice.) The entire way home, Kayla thought about sharing the good news with Mrs. Pennelly and getting her mother's advice on what to wear.

But when the bus pulled up at Kayla's house, she knew immediately that something was wrong. Normally, Rupert sat at attention as the bus stopped, then jumped up and down while Brian and Kayla descended to the yard. But looking through the bus window, Kayla realized that Rupert was gone. His broken chain laid curled in the dust beside the doghouse. As the bus creaked to a stop, Kayla heard desperate barking. Brian seemed unconcerned by the barking, but Kayla's heart beat fast as Mr. Tims lowered her down the steps.

As the bus pulled away, Rupert came tearing around the front of Mrs. Pennelly's house. At the same moment, their father's car pulled into the driveway. "Go get Dad," Kayla yelled to Brian as Rupert ran madly back toward Mrs. Pennelly's door. Realizing for the first time that something was wrong, Brian looked wide-eyed and scared. He raced to get his father while Kayla ran behind Rupert, forgetting the pain that normally slowed her movements.

Mrs. Pennelly's house seemed far too quiet as Kayla climbed the porch stairs two at a time and pushed open the front door. "Mrs. Pennelly?" she called into the house, fear adding a note of desperation to her voice. There was no answer, and Rupert pushed past Kayla's leg into the gray room.

The sound of her pounding blood filled Kayla's ears as she stepped over the threshold. Afternoon light streaked through the dusty air, momentarily blurring Kayla's vision. Rupert ran to the kitchen, and moving faster than she had in years, Kayla followed at his heels. She stopped abruptly at the kitchen door as a sharp pang slapped against her chest. She grabbed the doorframe with a white hand. Directly in front of her, she could see Mrs. Pennelly's feet extending from behind the kitchen's island. A cup of coffee stood untouched on the counter and a spoon lay a couple feet away on the floor.

Rupert whined, looking first at Mrs. Pennelly's feet, then at Kayla, then back again. Kayla cupped her hands around her mouth. A cry escaped her lips as she heard her father's feet pounding up the steps behind her.

That night, Kayla watched numbly from her bedroom window as Jermaine walked, hands in pockets, a slight swagger in his step, toward the front door. She could see three other figures in the car he'd left parked on the street. The three jumped out, leaving the doors open, ran around the car twice, then jumped back in and closed the doors behind them. She could hear their laughter and the faint sounds of her mother's voice at the door. Jermaine shifted his stance on the stoop, then turned and walked, shoulders slumped, back toward the car. One of the people in the back got out of the car and took the seat next to Jermaine up front. Kayla felt nothing as she watched them drive away.

SCHOOLS MEETING SPECIAL NEEDS

Students with chronic illnesses may require special services at their schools in order to learn and participate in school activities. Kayla, for example, needs to have daily physical therapy as well as a separate math class where she can catch up on material she has missed. Special exercise and tutorial classes are just some of the educational services that are especially important to students with chronic illness. Guidance counselors or school psychologists are also important resources for students. They are trained to help students through difficult times and adjustments. Students with a chronic illness will often have to take medicine during the school day. They may have special arrangements with the school health-care provider for taking medication. The people working in the school's health office should also have training to teach them about the specific needs of a student with a particular illness. At Kayla's school, her bus driver, physical therapy providers, teachers, and the other students all play roles in her support system.

Any student with a disability, including a chronic illness, is legally entitled to special support from the school system to assist with her education. Since 1973, a series of laws and court decisions have protected the rights of individuals with disabilities to fully participate in all aspects of our society. For instance, Section 504 of the Rehabilitation Act of 1973, a civil rights law, prohibits discrimination against individuals with disabilities, and provides "due process" where discrimination might have occurred. Then in 1975, the 94th Congress passed the landmark Education for the Handicapped Act, widely known as Public Law 94-142. Recently re-authorized as the Individuals with Disabilities Education Act (IDEA), this law provides states with federal funds to serve the needs of individuals with disabilities, ages three to twenty-one.

A student with a chronic illness is entitled to special support at school.

If a local school district cannot offer the services needed by a child with a disability, the district is required to provide the child with transportation to a school or other institution where those services will be available.

The school's swimming pool provides good exercise for children with special needs. Having access to physical education and enjoy the same school facilities as other students is just one aspect of a child's right to "an appropriate education" in the "least restrictive environment."

This is achieved through a very specific process defined within that law. *All* preschool and school-age students, regardless of the severity of their disability, must be provided an "appropriate education" in the "least restrictive environment." Each state has its own specific procedures, but at the minimum, a multidisciplinary team, which includes the parent, conducts an evaluation that identifies a student's eligibility and needs, and

Make Connections: Individualized Education Plan (IEP)

 An IEP is a written plan designed specifically for each child with special needs. It defines reasonable expectations for achievement and how success will be determined. It should include these points:

1. A statement of the child's current level of educational performance.
2. A statement of yearly goals or achievements expected for each area of identified weakness by the end of the school year.
3. Short-term objectives stated in instructional terms (concrete, observable steps leading to the mastery of the yearly goals).
4. A statement of the specific special education and support services to be provided to the child during the year covered by the IEP.
5. A statement of the extent to which a child will be able to participate in regular education programs and justification for any special placement recommended.
6. Projected dates for the beginning of services and how long they are anticipated to last.
7. A statement of the criteria and evaluation procedures to be used in determining (on at least an annual basis, if not more frequently) whether the short-term objectives have been achieved.

When an adolescent experiences a chronic illness, she may feel embarrassed or uncomfortable about interacting with her peers.

Research Project:

This chapter states that children with special needs are entitled to "an appropriate education in the least restrictive environment." Use the Internet or ask your librarian to help you find books that will help you understand exactly what these words mean. What are examples of an "appropriate education" for someone like Kayla? How might that be different from the "appropriate education" for a child who is blind or who has severe mental challenges? Give examples of how a "least restrictive environment" might look for each of these challenges. What might schools be required to do to ensure these rights?

uses an individualized education plan (IEP) to describe a program that meets that student's needs. To insure that the educational program is appropriate to the child's current (and evolving) needs, programs must be reviewed at least annually, with periodic reevaluations conducted at least every three years.

FITTING IN

Kayla is nervous at first about how her peers will react to the knowledge that she has a chronic illness. This is a common fear among young people with medical conditions. They may fear losing their friends, being laughed at, or just being treated differently from everyone else. Kayla finds, as many other students do, that her classmates are curious rather than judgmental about her illness. They want to help if they can, and a teacher offers to let Kayla give a presentation about her condition. The educational setting of a school is often a good place to discuss chronic illness, and many individuals find ways to use the classroom to teach their peers about their condition. Education is the best tool for fighting the **stereotypes** that people may have about chronic illness and breaking the barriers to social acceptance.

TYPES OF CHRONIC ILLNESSES: MULTIPLE SCLEROSIS

Often called MS, multiple sclerosis is a chronic illness of the central nervous system (the brain and spinal cord). With MS, a person's immune system over time attacks the protective tissue that surrounds nerve fibers. These fibers are responsible for transmitting messages between the brain, spinal cord, and the rest of the body.

For a person with MS, damage to the nervous system causes symptoms like loss of muscle coordination, muscle weakness, exhaustion, numbness, and tingling sensations.

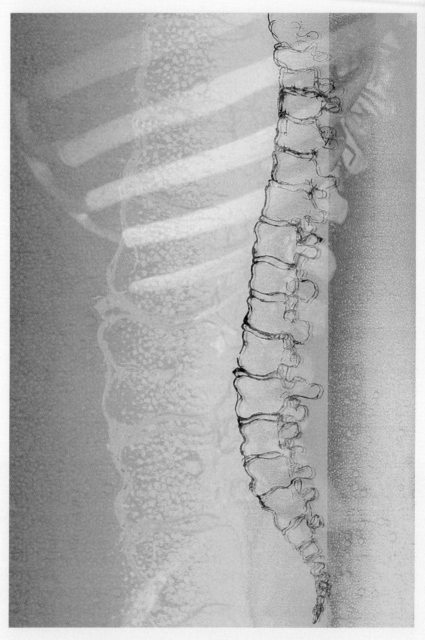

Multiple sclerosis affects the spinal cord.

The disease may progress slowly over time, with periods of few symptoms alternating with periods of severe symptoms. For other people, the disease may progress quickly, leading to the loss of balance and controlled movement, the ability to speak understandably, and the ability to be independent. Though treatments exist to help slow the progress of the disease, there is currently no cure for this debilitating condition. It is estimated that about 400,000 people in the United States have multiple sclerosis.

The only thing that can free you is the belief that you can be free.
—Oprah Winfrey

Words to Understand

relapse: A return to a previous state. Reverting back to pre-treatment conditions.
bacterium: A single-celled microorganism; may be beneficial or harmful to the body.

8

BREAKING THE CHAIN

After Mrs. Pennelly's death, Kayla suffered a serious *relapse*. As she had stood in the kitchen looking at Mrs. Pennelly's feet, all of the energy rushed from Kayla's body leaving her cold and empty. Her father had come, the ambulance was called, Mrs. Pennelly's funeral passed, and life began to return to normal, but the energy didn't come back. Every day that went by, Kayla felt like her body emptied a little more, and all the dark, hollow places filled up with pain. She began to secretly skip her medications and stopped going to Teens Talk. In the mornings, she was often too sick to get out of bed, and soon she was barely attending school.

The school psychologist and counselor made frequent calls to Kayla's parents, but her parents were unsure how to respond. Kayla did not want to talk to anyone, and she refused to keep the appointments with the counselor and psychologist. Her family had always worked together as a team to meet the challenges Kayla's illness posed, but now their most important fighter seemed to have given up.

Rupert had moved into the house with them after Mrs. Pennelly's death, and he barely ever left Kayla's side. Even this, however, failed to rouse Kayla from her frightening mood. As the days passed and Kayla's condition worsened, her parents realized that she was fighting a new enemy they had never seen before—hopelessness.

Deep down, Kayla knew she had the power to overcome this new stage of her illness; her relapse wasn't unconquerable.

Sometimes she lay in bed and tried to convince herself that she wanted to get up, that she'd like to go outside where she could feel the fresh air, sit with her family and talk about funny, meaningless things, climb out of this bed and go see a movie with Jermaine and his friends. But exhaustion rooted itself deep in her being. Her mind felt too heavy and slow to convince her body to roll out of bed. She knew her family was becoming more and more concerned, but she couldn't bring herself to care.

Everyone treaded carefully around Kayla, trying to be sensitive to her feelings, struggling to give her time to come to terms with whatever it was she was battling.

Everyone, that is, except Brian. With Kayla's new turn for the worse, he felt more left out than ever. It had been a long time since they'd been able to play and laugh the way they had before Kayla had gotten sick. Now summer was once again approaching, and Brian feared Kayla wouldn't be able to do any of the things she used to do with him, like taking Rupert for slow walks or going to the community pool to swim.

Brian's parents had warned him to give Kayla her space, but one day his frustration boiled to the surface and he stormed into his sister's bedroom. She was lying in bed, staring at the ceiling. She didn't even look at him as he came in.

Brian bounded over to Kayla's bed and flopped onto her patchwork quilt. The bed shook with his movement and aftershocks of pain rippled through Kayla's body. She would have yelled at Brian for this intrusion, but she didn't have the strength, so she just waited silently for the pain to subside.

"I know something," Brian stated. Kayla looked at her little brother, then back to the ceiling. Brian, however, wasn't going to be put off. "I know something you don't think I know." Kayla didn't stir. She didn't care what Brian thought he knew.

But then he continued. "Mom and Dad don't know why you're sick, but I know that you're not taking your medicine," Brian paused for effect. "I'm going to tell them."

Brian now had Kayla's attention. A feeling of desperation made the pain quicken in her chest. She looked urgently at her brother, unsure as to whether she should plead with him or threaten him, not confident that she had the strength to do either. She raised her head and grasped his arm. She thought she was going to yell, but the emotion turned unexpectedly to tears.

"Don't tell, Brian," was all she could manage around the lump in her throat. "Please don't tell."

Instead of being swayed to pity by his sister's emotions, Brian felt even angrier. He'd never stood up to his older sister before, and he didn't understand the new feeling that motivated him. "Why shouldn't I tell?" he yelled angrily, his strangled voice rising in the little room, "Why shouldn't I tell? You never do anything with me anymore! You're acting like a big baby!"

Brian gulped, trying to control the emotions that threatened to overwhelm him. "You're not my big sister at all anymore. You're just a big baby." He shook with the strength of his proclamation.

Kayla stared at her little brother in disbelief, then collapsed back on her pillow. How dare he say something like this to her, the little healthy brat! He had no idea what it was like to be her, to live with pain and exhaustion every day, to be sick if you didn't take your medicine, but sick in other ways if you did. He didn't know what it was like to have the only person who really understood you go and die, leaving you with no one to talk to anymore. He didn't know what it was like to be fifteen years old and not be able to go to a movie with your friends. He certainly didn't have a right to be judging her, claiming that being this sick was her fault.

Kayla hadn't understood before why she'd stopped taking her medication after Mrs. Pennelly died, but suddenly she knew. She looked at her little brother sniffling angrily beside her, all his emotions raw and unchecked on his face.

"You don't know anything, Brian," she informed him, the exhaustion evident in her voice. "Why should I spend all this time fighting and working and trying so hard when we all just go and die like Mrs. Pennelly?"

There. She had said it. Saying the words aloud was like a great weight lifting out of her body. Who could argue with that? No matter what she did, no matter how hard and how long she struggled, Kayla knew that some day she'd die . . . so what did it matter anyway?

Brian stared at his sister for a moment. "That's the stupidest thing I ever heard."

Kayla looked at her brother in shocked silence. How could he deny something so obvious? And, how could he sit there and tell her she was stupid? Brian, however, appeared to be unaffected by his sister's expression.

"Mrs. Pennelly was old. You're not," he stated flatly, then turned and left the room, leaving the truth of his words hanging in the air behind him.

Kayla stood in the open field, the yellow sun creating a halo of light around her body. The tall grasses brushed against her legs and the wind sang in her ears. Her feet floated effortlessly on the warm earth and her body hummed with a soft current of energy. A feeling of total well-being spread through her veins. Her blood pulsed contentment through every part of her body. She looked around at the never-ending field. She did not know this place, but it felt like home.

In the distance, she heard a dog barking, and she turned toward the sound. Her muscles moved smoothly and feather-light as they parted the yellow air. At the edge of the field, Rupert loped sleek and long through the swaying grass. Kayla's heart swelled to see him running free of his chain. As he came closer, Kayla had a sudden desire to run that fast and that free, and just as quickly as she had thought it, she felt her own body stretching across the field.

Suddenly, Kayla was running faster than she had ever dreamed. She could feel the wind pulling her hair back off her shoulders, pressing coolly against her skin, filling her lungs. Rupert quickened his pace beside her, spurring her to run faster, pushing her feet forward. Kayla gripped the soft earth with her toes, pulling it under her as she moved over it. Her body felt no pain, no discomfort, only moving muscles and power. She was master of the movement, master of everything. The ground sped away and the grasses whipped against her legs as her feet beat out a rhythm against the ground, a rhythm that sounded like music—like life. She wanted to run like this forever, free of the shackles of pain, with Rupert flying beside her unchained.

Intoxicated by the sense of freedom, Kayla did not see the dark hole welling in the ground ahead until it was too late. As her foot hit the empty air, she realized with horror that she was running too fast to stop. She felt herself falling, and the world went black.

Suddenly Kayla was straining in the dark. She was stuck in the narrow hole, her body wedged against the walls, dirt pushing against her on all sides. She pressed and wiggled as her muscles began to ache and pain constricted her chest; she tried to make herself long and skinny to slip out of her confinement. When that didn't work, she tried to make herself small. She puffed and scratched and struggled until she was so exhausted she couldn't move. For a moment she just lay there, beaten. Then the hole started to cave in. Dark earth crumbled down on her head. Rocks crushed her bones. The sides of the hole were collapsing, and Kayla knew she would suffocate. A whine rose around her as something wet pressed against her cheek.

Kayla opened her eyes and blinked into the morning light. The wetness pressed against her cheek again—Rupert. Kayla breathed a sigh of relief as her pounding heart began to slow. Standing beside her bed, the dog laid his head on Kayla's pillow and gave her a concerned look.

Kayla tried to swallow the fear that reverberated through her from the dream. She stared at the ceiling. As the light spread around her, she knew with a sudden certainty that if she did not get out of her bed today, she would never get well.

Kayla slipped her hand across the bed to Rupert's soft head. She took a deep breath. "Go get your leash Rupert," she said. Rupert raised his ears and made an expression that seemed unmistakably like pleasant surprise. Then he wheeled around and sped from the room. Kayla listened to his nails clicking down the hall and concentrated on gathering her strength.

She held the bedpost with determination and pulled herself up to sitting. Her muscles stretched and groaned. Leash in mouth, Rupert padded back into the room. "Good boy," Kayla praised. "It's gonna be slow," she warned, ruffling Rupert behind the ears, "but today we're going for a walk."

UNCERTAINTY ABOUT THE FUTURE

Uncertainty about the future can be a very painful emotional obstacle for young people with chronic illnesses. The fear of death is something that all people face, but people with chronic illnesses often struggle with an even more complicated fear—the fear of dying a premature death combined with the fear of living a painful life. Such confusing emotions can be an obstacle to anyone's attempts to stay healthy.

Many young people with chronic illness worry that they will not be able to lead a normal life, that they will not have successful romantic relationships, or even that their illness-stricken life will cease to be worth living. There are times when people struggling with long-term illnesses feel like

A young person with a chronic illness will experience many worries.

Individuals with a chronic illness can learn to rise above their disability.

Make Connections: More Than Medicine

Many people also seek to improve their quality of life with additions to their normal medical therapy. This may include joining support groups, becoming more involved in religious organizations, learning techniques like meditation to help control pain, and getting involved in community service or other activities that give the person a sense of purpose.

giving up. It is extremely important that individuals facing such emotions have people who they can talk to and who can give them guidance through difficult times. For many people with chronic illness, therapy with psychiatrists or psychologists becomes an important part of treatment.

TYPES OF CHRONIC ILLNESSES: LYME DISEASE

Although many chronic illnesses are genetically predetermined or develop for unknown reasons, some may be contracted from outside sources. Lyme disease, for instance, is an illness that is transmitted to people through the bite of an infected deer tick. If caught in its early stages, Lyme disease can be prevented from becoming a chronic disease, but if undiagnosed, it can have recurring symptoms that need regular treatment.

Lyme disease is caused by a **bacterium** called spirochete. When an infected tick bites a person, the spirochete bacteria infect the person's skin. The first symptoms of the infection are usually skin rashes, especially a rash about five to six

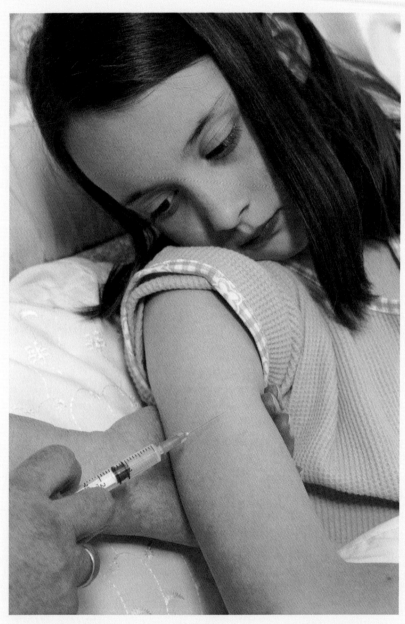

Having to receive frequent injections may be one of the difficulties of chronic illness.

inches (12.7 to 15.2 centimeters) across that looks like a bulls-eye.

If untreated, the bacteria spread to other tissues in the body. If Lyme disease progresses to a chronic stage, it causes symptoms like inflammation in one's joints, a stiff neck, tingling or numbness, and facial paralysis. In extreme cases, the disorder progresses to cause even more severe symptoms, like debilitating headaches, impaired concentration, heart problems, and even mental disorders.

Lyme disease is an illness that can often be prevented or treated before it becomes chronic. Wearing bug spray when spending time in areas like grassy fields (especially areas that have large numbers of deer and mice—the animals on which deer ticks are usually found) can help prevent ticks from biting. Checking yourself for ticks after being outside is another good precaution. Should you be bitten by a tick and develop a rash as a result, see a doctor immediately.

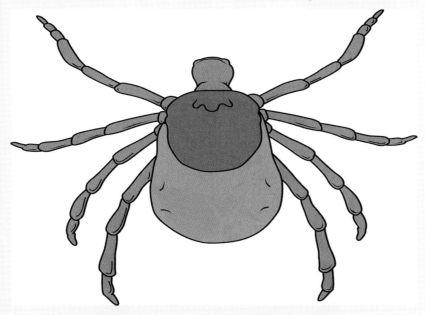

Lyme disease is caused by bacteria carried by ticks.

Research Project:

Find out more about Lyme disease using the library or Internet. How did it get its name? How long have doctors known about this disease? How many people get it each year? How is it treated?

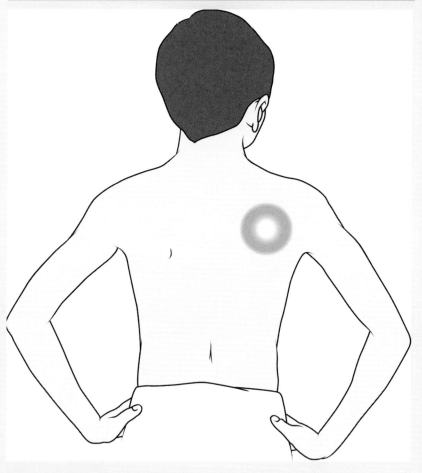

The first symptom of Lyme disease is a distinctive "bulls-eye" rash.

Text-Dependent Questions

1. How has Kayla changed at the end of this book from the person she was at the beginning? What are some of the stages that she passed through along the way?
2. What are some of the worries that young people with chronic illnesses may experience?
3. List some of the things besides medicine that may help people with chronic illnesses.
4. What causes Lyme disease? What are its first symptoms? What are later symptoms?
5. How can Lyme disease be prevented?

Treating Lyme disease in its early stages can prevent the development of long-lasting symptoms.

EACH DAY IS A GIFT!

Despite the difficult times that people with chronic illness inevitably face, many people say that living with a disease has taught them to see every single day as a gift. In some ways, having a chronic illness may make a person more determined to enjoy every day that they are given.

FURTHER READING

Berger, William E. *Living with Asthma*. New York: Checkmark Books, 2008.

Donoghue, Paul J. *Sick and Tired of Feeling Sick and Tired: Living with Invisible Chronic Illness*. New York: Norton, 2012.

Fadiman, Anne. *The Spirit Catches You and You Fall Down: A Hmong Child, Her American Doctors, and the Collision of Two Cultures*. New York: Farrar, Straus, and Giroux, 2012.

Lorig, Kate. *Living a Healthy Life with Chronic Conditions: Self-Management of Heart Disease, Arthritis, Diabetes, Depression, Asthma, Bronchitis, Emphysema and Other Physical and Mental Health Conditions*. Boulder, CO: Bull, 2012.

Schoch, Jen. *Lupus And Me: Living Well With An Autoimmune Illness*. Seattle, OR: CreateSpace, 2013.

Wallace, Daniel J. *The Lupus Book: A Guide for Patients and Their Families, Revised and Expanded Edition*. New York: Oxford University Press, 2012.

FOR MORE INFORMATION

Acne.org
www.acne.org

The American Chronic Pain Association
www.theacpa.org

American Lyme Disease Foundation
www.aldf.com

Arthritis Foundation
www.arthritis.org

Chronic Fatigue Syndrome
The CFIDS Association of America
www.cfids.org

Eczema Information
www.nationaleczema.org

Epilepsy Foundation of America
www.efa.org

Lupus Canada
www.lupuscanada.org

The Lupus Foundation of America
www.lupus.org

National Library of Medicine
www.nlm.nih.gov

National Multiple Sclerosis Society
www.nmss.org

National Organization for Rare Diseases
www.rarediseases.org

National Vitiligo Foundation
www.mynvfi.org

Publisher's Note:

The websites listed on these pages were active at the time of publication. The publisher is not responsible for websites that have changed their address or discontinued operation since the date of publication. The publisher will review and update the websites upon each reprint.

SERIES GLOSSARY
OF KEY TERMS

Accessibility: An environment that allows people with disabilities to participate as much as they can.

Accommodation: A change in how a student receives instruction, without substantially changing the instructional content.

Achievement test: A standardized test that measures a student's performance in academic areas such as math, reading, and writing.

Acting out: Behavior that's inappropriate within the setting.

Adaptive behavior: The extent to which an individual is able to adjust to and apply new skills to new environments, tasks, objects, and people.

Ambulatory: Able to walk independently.

American Sign Language (ASL): A language based on gestures that is used by people who are deaf in the United States and Canada.

Americans with Disabilities Act (ADA): In 1990, Congress passed this act, which provides people who have disabilities with the same freedoms as Americans who do not have disabilities. The law addresses access to buildings and programs, as well as housing and employment.

Anxiety: An emotional state of fear, often not attached to any direct threat, which can cause sweating, increased pulse, and breathing difficulty.

Aphasia: Loss of the ability to speak.

Articulation: The ability to express oneself through sounds, words, and sentences.

Asperger syndrome: An disorder that is on the autism spectrum, which can cause problems with nonverbal learning disorder and social interactions.

Assessment: The process of collecting information about a student's learning needs through tests, observations, and interviewing the student, the family, and others. Assistive technology: Any item or piece of equipment that is used to improve the capabilities of a child with a disability.

Attention-deficit/hyperactivity Disorder (ADHD): A disorder that can cause inappropriate behavior, including poor attention skills, impulsivity, and hyperactivity.

Autism spectrum disorder: A range of disabilities that affect verbal and nonverbal communication and social interactions.

Bipolar disorder: A brain disorder that causes uncontrollable changes in moods, behaviors, thoughts, and activities.

Blind (legally): Visual acuity for distance vision of 20/200 or less in the better eye after best correction with conventional lenses; or a visual field of no greater than 20 degrees in the better eye.

Bullying: When a child faces threats, intimidation, name-calling, gossip, or physical violence.

Cerebral palsy (CP): Motor impairment caused by brain damage during birth or before birth. It can be mild to severe, does not get worse, and cannot be cured. Chronic: A condition that persists over a long period of time.

Cognitive: Having to do with remembering, reasoning, understanding, and using judgment.

Congenital: Any condition that is present at birth.

Counseling: Advice or help through talking, given by someone qualified to give such help.

Deaf: A hearing loss so severe that speech cannot be understood, even with a hearing aid, even if some sounds may still be perceived.

Developmental: Having to do with the steps or stages in growth and development of a child.

Disability: A limitation that interferes with a person's ability to walk, hear, talk, or learn.

Down syndrome: An abnormal chromosomal condition that changes the development of the body and brain, often causing intellectual disabilities.

Early intervention: Services provided to infants and toddlers ages birth to three who are at risk for or are showing signs of having a slower than usual development.

Emotional disturbance (ED): An educational term (rather than psychological) where a student's inability to build or maintain satisfactory interpersonal relationships with peers and teachers, inappropriate types of behavior or feelings, and moods of unhappiness or depression get in the way of the student being able to learn and function in a school setting.

Epilepsy: A brain disorder where the electrical signals in the brain are disrupted, causing seizures. Seizures can cause brief changes in a person's body movements, awareness, emotions, and senses (such as taste, smell, vision, or hearing).

Fine motor skills: Control of small muscles in the hands and fingers, which are needed for activities such as writing and cutting.

Gross motor skills: Control of large muscles in the arms, legs, and torso, which are needed for activities such as running and walking.

Hard-of-hearing: A hearing loss that may affect the student's educational performance.

Heredity: Traits acquired from parents.

Individualized Education Plan (IEP): A written education plan for students ages 5 to 22 with disabilities, developed by a team of professionals, (teachers, therapists, etc.) and the child's parent(s), which is reviewed and updated yearly. It contains a description of the child's level of development, learning needs, goals and objectives, and services the child will receive.

Individuals with Disabilities Education Act (IDEA): The Individuals with Disabilities Education Act (IDEA) is the nation's federal special education law that requires public schools to serve the educational needs of students with disabilities. IDEA requires that schools provide special education services to eligible students as outlined in a student's IEP, and it also provides very specific requirements to guarantee a free appropriate education for students with disabilities in the least restrictive environment.

Intervention: A planned activity to increase students' skills.

Learning disability: A general term for specific kinds of learning problems that can cause a person to have challenges learning and using certain skills, such as reading, writing, listening, speaking, reasoning, and doing math.

Least restrictive environment: The educational setting or program that provides a student with as much contact as possible with children without disabilities, while still appropriately meeting all of the child's learning and physical needs.

Mainstreaming: Providing any services, including education, for children with disabilities, in a setting with other children who do not have disabilities.

Motor: Having to do with muscular activity.

Nonambulatory: Not able to walk independently.

Occupational therapist (OT): A professional who helps individuals be able to handle meaningful activities of daily life such as self-care skills, education, recreation, work or social interaction.

Palate: The roof of the mouth.

Paraplegia: Paralysis of the legs and lower part of the body.

Partially sighted: A term formally used to indicate visual acuity of 20/70 to 20/200, but also used to describe visual impairment in which usable vision is present.

Pediatrics: The medical treatment of children.

Physical therapist (PT): A person who helps individuals improve the use of bones, muscles, joints, and/or nerves.

Prenatal: Existing or occurring prior to birth.

Quadriplegia: Paralysis affecting all four limbs.

Referral: In special education, students are referred for screening and evaluation to see if they are eligible for special education services.

Self-care skills: The ability to care for oneself; usually refers to basic habits of dressing, eating, etc.

Special Education: Specialized instruction made to fit the unique learning strengths and needs of each student with disabilities in the least restrictive environment.

Speech impaired: Communication disorder such as stuttering, impaired articulation, a language impairment, or a voice impairment, which adversely affects a child's educational performance.

Speech pathologist: A trained therapist, who provides treatment to help a person develop or improve articulation, communication skills, and oral-motor skills.

Spina bifida: A problem that happens in the first month of pregnancy when the spinal column doesn't close completely.

Standardized tests: Tests that use consistent directions, procedures, and criteria for scoring, which are often administered to many students in many schools across the country.

Stereotyping: A generalization in which individuals are falsely assigned traits they do not possess based on race, ethnicity, religion, disability, or gender.

Symptom: An observable sign of an illness or disorder.

Syndrome: A set of symptoms that occur together.

Therapy: The treatment or application of different techniques to improve specific conditions for curing or helping to live with various disorders.

Traumatic Brain Injury (TBI): Physical damage to the brain that could result in physical, behavioral, or mental changes depending on which area of the brain is injured.

Visually impaired: Any degree of vision loss that affects an individual's ability to perform the tasks of daily life, which is caused by a visual system that is not working properly or not formed correctly.

Vocational education: Educational programs that prepare students for paid or unpaid employment, or which provide additional preparation for a career that doesn't require a college degree.

INDEX